GROW SERIES

WALK WITH GOD

A PRACTICAL GUIDE TO FOLLOWING CHRIST

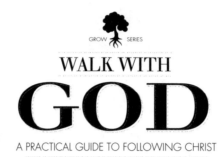

WALK WITH
GOD

A PRACTICAL GUIDE TO FOLLOWING CHRIST

Copyright 2017 – Craig Etheredge. All rights reserved.

Published by **discipleFIRST**
5405 Pleasant Run, Colleyville, TX 76034

Unless otherwise noted, scripture quotations are from the ESV® Bible
(The Holy Bible, English Standard Version®), copyright © 2001 by
Crossway, a publishing ministry of Good News Publishers. Used by permission.
All rights reserved.

Scripture quotations marked NLT are taken from the Holy Bible,
New Living Translation, copyright © 1996. Used by permission of
Tyndale House Publishers, Inc., Wheaton, Illinois 60189. All rights reserved.

Scripture quotations marked (NLT) are taken from the Holy Bible,
New Living Translation, copyright ©1996, 2004, 2007, 2013 by
Tyndale House Foundation. Used by permission of Tyndale House
Publishers, Inc., Carol Stream, Illinois 60188. All rights reserved.

ISBN: 978-0-9993439-1-3

PRINTED IN THE UNITED STATES OF AMERICA

Book Design and Layout: Kim Slater - katCreative.net

First Edition

DEDICATION

To the team of pastors at First Colleyville who relentlessly pursue God and challenge me to do the same.

Unlock this digital resource in the

Learn more at **discipleFIRST.com/app**

TABLE OF CONTENTS

1
FOLLOWING JESUS

27
JESUS AT THE CENTER

49
LISTENING TO GOD

71
TALKING TO GOD

101
OBEYING GOD

131
GOD'S AMAZING GRACE

165
CONNECTING WITH GOD'S FAMILY

I
APPENDIX

HOW TO USE THIS BOOK

Every long journey starts with the first step, and today you are taking an important step to learn how to walk with God in a deep and personal way. The things you are going to read in this book are not new. In fact, I'm simply passing on to you lessons taught to me by godly men and women who invested in my life over the years. Chances are good that they learned from others who went before them, so you are standing in a long line of godly people who — from generation to generation — have sought to know God and walk with Him. As you begin to move through this book, I want to point out a few features that will help you get the most out of your experience.

This book is comprised of seven chapters, each explaining a fundamental theme about how to walk with God. While a mountain of books could be written on how to walk with God, my experience is that these seven truths provide the necessary foundation for any healthy relationship with God. Also, these chapters are presented in a specific, logical order so that each week builds upon the previous one, unfolding practical things you can do to draw closer to God. I recommend that you take one chapter a week and focus on putting what you learn into practice.

You will notice that each chapter is broken down into seven daily readings. These readings are not long and should only take a few minutes each day. At the end of each reading, a few reflective questions are included under the heading "Think It Out." Take a minute to write down your answers to these questions. The more you stop to think about what you just read and take the time to write down your thoughts, the more you will get out of each reading. You will also find at the end of each daily reading a section called "Live It Out," which will give you something practical to do that day to help you walk with God.

In addition, each chapter includes a memory verse located at the chapter break. Over the centuries, godly people have memorized Scripture to help them walk with God. I want to encourage you to memorize the verse for the week. On page iv, you will find a guide on how to most effectively memorize Scripture. If you are not a big memorization fan, don't worry. The verses are short, but their impact is huge!

Lastly, I want to encourage you to take this journey with someone else. We always learn better in a group of people all pursuing the same goal. For best results, I recommend you gather with a group of two to four people and talk about what you learn each week and how you are putting it into practice.

A group is best because you can learn from each other's insights. You can pray for each other. You can hold each other accountable to read God's Word and memorize Scripture. Most of all, you can encourage each other to keep pursuing God, especially when times get tough. The end of each chapter includes places to write down reflections from your group experience as well as one thing you will do as a result of what you learned together.

The next seven weeks of your life are going to be amazing. This book you are holding in your hand was written for you. I sincerely believe that if your desire is to know God and walk with Him, then this practical guide will help you accomplish just that. **(James 4.8 NLT)** says, *"Come close to God and he will come close to you."* As you begin each day coming close to God through reading His Word and seeking Him, I know that He will come close to you!

Let's get started!

Craig

BIBLE TRANSLATIONS

AMPC: Amplified Classic Bible
ESV: English Standard Version
JBP: J.B. Phillips New Testament
NASB: New American Standard Bible
NIV: New International Version
NLT: New Living Translation
TLB: The Living Bible

MEMORIZING SCRIPTURE

"How can a young man keep his way pure? By guarding it according to your word. ...I have stored up your word in my heart, that I might not sin against you." **(Psalm 119.9, 11 ESV)**

WHY MEMORIZE SCRIPTURE?

Scripture memory is foundational to your spiritual growth in Christ. Jesus Himself knew the Scriptures by memory. As a young Jewish boy, He would have been required to memorize the first five books of the Old Testament (Torah) by His twelfth birthday. Throughout Jesus' ministry He quoted Scripture from memory eighty different times from seventy different passages. He quoted the Scriptures from memory, saying three times *"it is written"* as He resisted temptation **(Matthew 4.1-11)**.

His disciples were also devoted to God's Word and gave their full attention to prayer and preaching the Scriptures **(Acts 2.42, 6.4)**. Over the centuries, great men and women of God have given their attention to memorizing God's Word.

"Bible memorization is absolutely fundamental to spiritual formation. If I had to choose between all the disciplines of the spiritual life, I would choose Bible memorization, because it is a fundamental way of filling our mind with what it needs. This book of the law shall not depart out of your mouth. That's where you need it! How does it get in your mouth? Memorization."

— **Dallas Willard**, Professor of Philosophy at the University of Southern California

(*"Spiritual Formation in Christ for the Whole Life and Whole Person"* in Vocatio, Vol. 12, No. 2, Spring 2001, p. 7.)

"I know of no other single practice in the Christian life more rewarding, practically speaking, than memorizing Scripture. …No other single exercise pays greater spiritual dividends! Your prayer life will be strengthened. Your witnessing will be sharper and much more effective. Your attitudes and outlook will begin to change. Your mind will become alert and observant. Your confidence and assurance will be enhanced. Your faith will be solidified."

— **Chuck Swindoll**, Chancellor of Dallas Theological Seminary
(Growing Strong in the Seasons of Life, Grand Rapids: Zondervan, 1994, p. 61.)

BEFORE YOU START

- Gather the right materials. You will need a Scripture memory card, a Scripture memory packet, a pen and a Bible.
- Choose a passage that is in a version you can easily understand and memorize.
- Read the context of the verse so you fully understand its meaning.
- Write the verse on one side of your Scripture memory card and the citation (where the verse is found) on the other side.

> John 3.16 NIV
>
> January 1, 2017

> For God so loved the world that he gave his one and only Son, that whoever believes in him shall not perish but have eternal life.

MEMORIZING YOUR VERSE

- Read the verse out loud eight to ten times.
- Break down the verse into phrases. Practice reciting the first phrase multiple times until you have it from memory. Then add the next phrase until you have it by memory. Continue until you can perfectly recite the verse word for word from memory.
- Be sure to memorize the citations of the verse (ex: **JOHN 3.16**), not just the verse itself.
- Think deeply about each phrase as you memorize it. How does this apply to your life? Go beyond memorizing it, and let it sink down into your heart.

HOW TO KEEP IT

- Keep your cards together in your Scripture memory packet.
- Review. Review. Review. Repetition etches the verses in your mind and heart.
- Find a friend or family member who will check you on your verses.
- Share your verse with a friend. As you use it to encourage others, God will encourage you.

WEEKLY MEMORY VERSES

WEEK ONE

"For God so loved the world that he gave his one and only Son, that whoever believes in him shall not perish but have eternal life," **(JOHN 3.16 NIV)**.

WEEK TWO

But seek first the kingdom of God and his righteousness, and all these things will be added to you," **(MATTHEW 6.33 ESV)**.

WEEK THREE

"My sheep listen to my voice, I know them and they follow me..." **(JOHN 10.27 NIV)**.

WEEK FOUR

"My heart says of you, 'Seek his face!' Your face, LORD, I will seek," **(PSALM 27.8 NIV)**.

WEEK FIVE

"Whoever has my commandments and keeps them, he it is who loves me. And he who loves me will be loved by my Father, and I will love him and manifest myself to him," **(JOHN 14.21 ESV)**.

WEEK SIX

"For it is by grace you have been saved, through faith – and this is not from yourselves, it is the gift of God – not by works, so that no one can boast," **(EPHESIANS 2.8-9 NIV)**.

WEEK SEVEN

"... you are no longer foreigners and strangers, but fellow citizens with God's people and also members of his household..." **(EPHESIANS 2.19 NIV)**.

"I WILL" COMMITMENT

Anything worthwhile requires a commitment, and the same is true in your walk with God. Jesus never shied away from asking people for a commitment. When He recruited men and women, He often said, *"Follow Me."* The words literally mean, *"Follow in my steps. Walk the way I'm walking."* It was a commitment to do something. I really believe you will never walk with God deeply until you make a commitment to follow Him completely. Over the next seven weeks, you are going to be challenged to put into practice what you are learning. Each week you will craft an **"I Will"** statement that makes a commitment to do something you learned that week. So before you take this journey, now would be a good time to make your first **"I Will"** commitment. It's a commitment to walk this walk, to take the journey and see what God has for you. Take a moment and reflect on the following commitments. If you are ready to take the challenge, check each box and sign your name at the bottom.

☐ I will read each day with an open heart that's eager to hear from God.

☐ I will enlist someone to pray with me and for me, as I take this journey.

☐ I will gather with my group and grow together.

☐ I will do what's assigned to me, knowing that this will help me to know God better.

Signature _____

FOLLOWING
JESUS

WEEK ONE

▶ **MEMORY VERSE**

"For God so loved the world that he gave his one and only Son, that whoever believes in him shall not perish but have eternal life."

(JOHN 3.16 NIV)

WEEK **ONE** · DAY **ONE**

THE GREAT ADVENTURE

Jesus gave the same invitation to everyone. It was simple, direct and called for a decision. It could be accepted or denied, but not ignored. The invitation was simply, *"Follow me."* More than twenty-four times in the Gospels, Jesus invited people to follow Him. He invited the wealthy and powerful, the casual observer, the spiritual seekers, and even the religiously devoted. Jesus called everyone to follow Him.

One day while walking along the Sea of Galilee, Jesus passed by fishermen caring for their nets. They had known Jesus for a while, but now it was time for them to make a decision.

> *"And he said to them, 'Follow me, and I will make you fishers of men'."*
> **(MATTHEW 4.19 ESV)**

For those men, following Jesus meant leaving behind their old life to go with Jesus. It meant being trained by Jesus, learning to obey Jesus, and coming under the authority and leadership of Jesus. Ultimately, it meant living a life that looked just like Jesus — reflecting His character, priorities and practices. Jesus offers the same invitation today. He still calls men and women to follow Him.

While following Jesus doesn't mean physically following Him around, it does mean turning from living your own life and choosing to live a new kind of life with Jesus in charge. Essentially, there are two ways to live. You can live with yourself in charge, going your way and pursuing your own happiness. Or you can live with Jesus in charge, going His way and pursuing what makes Him happy. This week you will discover that the first way to live always leads to a dead end and separation from God, while the second way always leads to purpose, peace and assurance.

THINK IT OUT

What do you think it means to follow Jesus today?

___

___

___

___

Why do some people not want to live with Jesus in charge?

___

___

___

___

LIVE IT OUT

Begin memorizing your Scripture memory verse for the week:

"For God so loved the world, that he gave his one and only Son, that whoever believes in him shall not perish but have eternal life."

(JOHN 3.16 NIV)

PRAY IT OUT

Ask Him to help you know Him better today.

WEEK **ONE** · DAY **TWO**

THE PATH

I will never forget climbing my first 14,000-foot peak in Colorado. At the beginning, the path was very clear and obvious. The trailhead parking lot was full of cars, signs were everywhere, and people busily milled about. The path seemed worn and gradual as we trekked through tall pine trees and past mountain meadows. I thought to myself, *"This is going to be easy!"*

As we started to switchback up the mountain and the grade became steeper, I could tell I was in for a hard day's work. Once we cleared the tree line, the path all but disappeared. Only stacked stones called cairns marked the path to the summit. At one point we thought we could see the summit and left the path for a shortcut up one face of the mountain, only to find that it led to a false summit and some pretty treacherous cliffs. We had to cautiously backtrack several miles to return to the right path. Ultimately, we made it to the top — exhausted but victorious!

I learned a life lesson that day that has stayed with me all these years: The path you choose determines your destination. Think about taking a trip. If you live in Dallas and want to take your family to the sunny beaches of San Diego, you don't get on Interstate 20 heading east. You might make it to Atlanta, but no matter how well-intentioned you may be or how badly you want to be in California, you would never get to San Diego. Why? The path you chose didn't lead there. That day on the mountain, we thought we could take a different path and get to the summit, but we were wrong. In the same way, the path you choose in life will determine your destination.

God created you to know Him personally and walk with Him along the path He has for you. The Bible calls this the path of life. *"You make known to me the path of life; in your presence there is fullness of joy; at your right hand are pleasures forevermore,"* **(Psalm 16.11 ESV)**.

Along this path you will find *"fullness of joy"* in God's presence and experience all the good things He has for you. At the very beginning of creation, God made all things, and He made them all good, **(Genesis 1.31 ESV)**. The first people God made enjoyed a perfect relationship with Him. They knew God. In **(John 17.3 NLT)** Jesus said, *"And this is the way to have eternal life — to know you, the only true God, and Jesus Christ, the one you sent to earth."* The word *"know"* doesn't just mean to know facts about something; it means to have an intimate personal knowledge of someone. That's why God created you — to know Him.

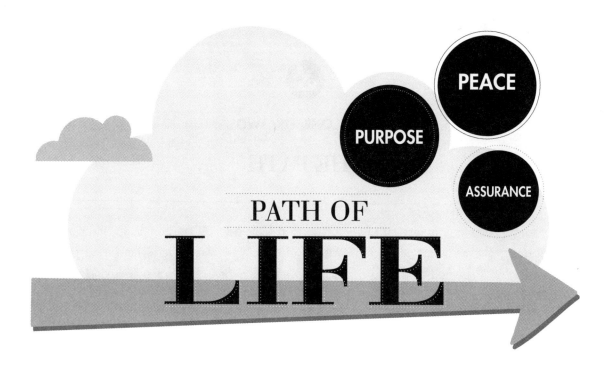

Along this path God promises purpose, peace and assurance. Purpose means that along this path of life, you will discover who you are, and how you can fulfill the purpose God has for your life. Peace means that on this path you will find peace with God and the secret to peace with other people. Assurance means that along this path, you can know with confidence that you will spend eternity with God in heaven.

THINK IT OUT

Do you agree with the statement, *"The path you choose determines your destination"*? Why or why not?

_____
_____
_____
_____
_____

Where is the path you've chosen leading you right now?

_____
_____
_____
_____

If God created you to know Him deeply and personally, then what does this tell you about God? What does this tell you about you?

_____
_____
_____
_____
_____
_____
_____

LIVE IT OUT

Review your Scripture memory verse for the week:

"For God so loved the world, that he gave his one and only Son, that whoever believes in him shall not perish but have eternal life."

(JOHN 3.16 NIV)

PRAY IT OUT

Thank God that He has a path for your life. Ask Him to help you know Him better today.

WEEK **ONE** · DAY **THREE**

DETOUR

Don't you hate detours? One minute you are headed down the road making good time and then suddenly, you see orange cones and flashing signs reading, *"Detour Ahead."* Usually a detour means going out of the way and wasting time. Sometimes it actually leads you in the opposite direction from where you want to go.

Whether you know it or not, your life has been detoured. Yesterday, we saw that God created everything good, and the first people God made experienced His presence and joy every day. Unfortunately, most people are not experiencing God like that today. Why? Because something happened that diverted us from God's path. That something is our own waywardness.

Although God has a path that is perfect, we have an innate desire to go our own way, do our own thing and go off-road from God's path. The prophet Isaiah put it this way: *"All we like sheep have gone astray; we have turned — every one — to his own way..."* **(Isaiah 53.6 ESV)**. The Bible calls this straying away *"sin."*

Sin is disobeying and going against God's direction for our lives. Ultimately, sin is cosmic treason; choosing to live for myself rather than live for the God who created me, knows me and loves me. Originally, sin was an archery term used to describe an archer who missed the bull's-eye, and in our own way, we each have missed the mark of God's created design. We have gone astray. We have taken a turn for the worse. We have left God's path to forge our own way.

The first person God made was Adam. Although Adam knew and walked with God, he chose to disobey Him, and as a result sin came into the world. **(Romans 5.12 NLT)** says, *"When Adam sinned, sin entered the world. Adam's sin brought death, so death spread to everyone, for everyone sinned."* Consequently, all of us now have a selfish and sinful bent to go astray from God. Just like a wheel that's been knocked out of alignment and now pulls to one side, our natural bent is to pull away from God.

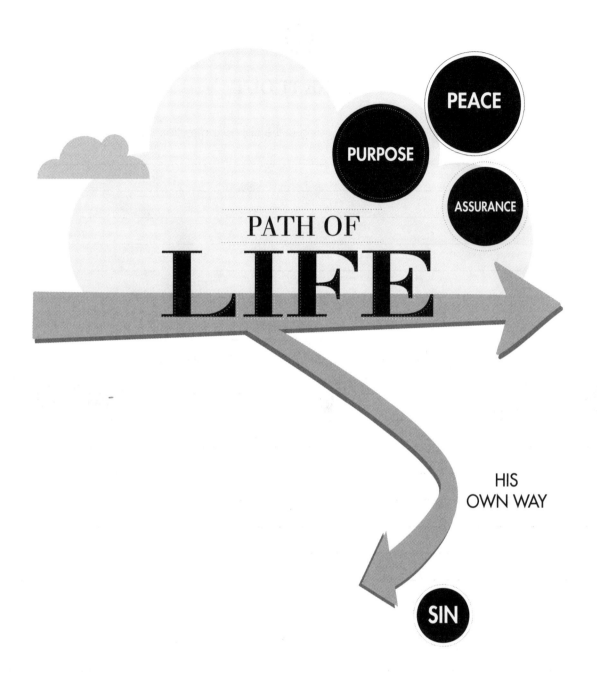

(Romans 3.23 NLT) says, *"For everyone has sinned; we all fall short of God's glorious standard."* Notice the word *"everyone."* That includes you. All of us have chosen to go our own way. Consequently, we live in a world that has lost its way and is headed in the wrong direction, leaving pain and misery in its wake. While following our own path may look good at first, ultimately it only leads to a dead end and isolation from God.

THINK IT OUT

In what ways do you see our culture going in the opposite direction from God's path?

_____
_____
_____
_____
_____
_____

According to this study, what is the source of evil and pain in our world?

_____
_____
_____
_____
_____
_____
_____
_____

How has your life taken a detour from God's path?

_____
_____
_____
_____
_____
_____
_____

What were some of the signs that you were headed in the wrong direction?

_____
_____
_____
_____
_____
_____
_____

If the people you know are truly headed in the wrong direction, then what is their greatest need?

_____
_____
_____
_____
_____

LIVE IT OUT

Review your Scripture memory verse for the week:

"For God so loved the world, that he gave his one and only Son, that whoever believes in him shall not perish but have eternal life."
(JOHN 3.16 NIV)

PRAY IT OUT

Thank God that He saw you and rescued you when you were going in the wrong direction.

WEEK **ONE** · DAY **FOUR**

HITTING THE WALL

Nobody likes hitting the wall. Athletes hit the wall when they can't go any farther. Students hit the wall when they can't study any more. When you and I make the decision to go our own way, leaving God's path to chart our own, it always results in hitting the wall.

Usually this comes in the form of some crisis or difficulty. Sometimes it comes in a feeling of loneliness or desperation. Often it comes in a quiet sense that we are far from God, and we don't know how to get back. Suddenly, we realize we are not living out God's intended purpose for our lives. We recognize we don't have peace with God or with people. We acknowledge that we don't have assurance that when we die, we are going to heaven. It is then that we understand the road we have taken has led to a dead end, and we are isolated from God.

The prophet Isaiah wrote: *"But your iniquities have separated you from your God; your sins have hidden his face from you, so that he will not hear,"* **(Isaiah 59.2 NIV)**. Sin always leads to separation. At some point, you may try to do things to get yourself back on track with God. You may try being a better person, doing good things for people, even becoming more religious, but nothing can change your situation. Again, Isaiah wrote: *"We are all infected and impure with sin. When we display our righteous deeds, they are nothing but filthy rags,"* **(Isaiah 64.6 NLT)**. Even our best isn't good enough.

When you turned to go your own way, you turned your back on God. But in His love and kindness, God didn't turn His back on you. He will often bring you to the place where you realize how far you've drifted.

Hitting the wall is actually a good thing because it awakens you to your desperate need for God, and gives you a chance to make a course correction. However, if anyone stubbornly continues to go down the wrong road, ultimately that person will hit the wall of God's justice. **(Romans 14.12 NLT)** says, *"Yes, each of us will give a personal account to God."* Those who are found guilty of sin and refuse to turn to God will experience God's justice.

(Nahum 1.3 NLT) says, *"The LORD is slow to get angry, but his power is great, and he never lets the guilty go unpunished."* Because God is just, He cannot tolerate injustice. Because He is holy, He cannot ignore sin. What is the punishment for sin? **(Romans 6.23 ESV)** begins with these startling words: *"For the wages of sin is death."* The punishment for our sin and waywardness is not just physical death, but spiritual death and separation from God forever. This is the bad news of the Bible. We've lost our way, and we are powerless to get back on our own.

THINK IT OUT

Why is it necessary for God to punish sin?

_____
_____
_____
_____
_____
_____
_____
_____
_____
_____
_____

Why is being good never good enough to make us right with God?

_____
_____
_____
_____
_____
_____
_____
_____
_____
_____

Have you ever come to a place where you hit the wall and realized you were far from God? Explain.

_____
_____
_____
_____
_____
_____
_____
_____
_____
_____

LIVE IT OUT

Review your Scripture memory verse for the week:

"For God so loved the world, that he gave his one and only Son, that whoever believes in him shall not perish but have eternal life."
(JOHN 3.16 NIV)

PRAY IT OUT

Take time to praise God for both His justice and His mercy.

WEEK **ONE** · DAY **FIVE**

THE CROSS

Heroes come at just the right time. Just when the situation looks the bleakest or the odds of a rescue are down to nothing, that's when a hero shows up! In a very real way that is what we needed. We needed a hero — someone who would step in and rescue us as we raced like crash dummies toward the wall of God's justice. And that is exactly what God did through His Son, Jesus.

When there was no hope — and at just the right time — Jesus came into the world, **(Romans 5.6 ESV)**. Though Jesus was by nature fully God, He set aside His eternal glory and was born as a baby, **(Philippians 2.6-8 ESV)**. He grew up just like you and me. He experienced temptation and pain, heartache and betrayal. He lived our life, yet He did it without sin. He never veered off course from His heavenly Father's will, **(Hebrews 4.15 ESV)**. He lived the life we were meant to live, walking the path of life and enjoying His Father's presence, just as we were designed to do.

Because He was perfect in every way, Jesus could now step in as a substitute for you and me and pay for our sin. In His ultimate act of love, Jesus was crucified and died on a cross for our sin, paying our punishment in full.

Think about it. All our sin was rolled onto the back of innocent Jesus, and God the Father treated Him just as if He had sinned our sin, **(2 Corinthians 5.21 ESV)**. He bore your sin and mine on that cross, suffering God's wrath against sin. From the cross He cried out *"tetelestai,"* which means *"it is complete"* or *"paid in full,"* **(John 19.30 ESV)**. These were the words a merchant would stamp on a receipt to prove the debt was paid. That is what Jesus did for you. He paid your sin debt in full so you could be forgiven and start over.

(Romans 6.23 NLT) says, *"For the wages of sin is death, but the free gift of God is eternal life through Jesus Christ our Lord."* Jesus died on a cross, and His body was buried in a borrowed tomb. Three days later He rose from the dead, conquering sin and death. After His resurrection, He appeared to hundreds of people over a forty-day period, proving Himself to be alive, **(Acts 1.3 ESV)**.

(1 Peter 3.18 NLT) says, *"Christ suffered for our sins once for all time. He never sinned, but he died for sinners to bring you safely home to God."* Jesus did what our own good works could never do — He made a way for us to get back to God.

Hearing all that Jesus has done, anyone would wonder, *"Why?"* Why did Jesus do all of this for you and me? One word: love. **(John 3.16 ESV)** says, *"For God so loved the world, that he gave his only Son, that whoever believes in him should not perish but have eternal life."* You could scratch out the word *"world"* and put your name in its place.

God sent His Son, Jesus, on a rescue mission from heaven just for you! That's incredible love. That's an incredible hero.

THINK IT OUT

According to our study, what made Jesus different from anyone else?

_____
_____
_____
_____
_____
_____
_____
_____
_____
_____

Why did Jesus die on the cross?

_____
_____
_____
_____
_____
_____
_____
_____
_____
_____
_____
_____

What does this tell you about how God feels about you?

_____
_____
_____
_____
_____
_____
_____
_____
_____
_____
_____
_____

LIVE IT OUT

Review your Scripture memory verse for the week:

"For God so loved the world, that he gave his one and only Son, that whoever believes in him shall not perish but have eternal life."
(JOHN 3.16 NIV)

PRAY IT OUT

Take time to praise God for sending Jesus to die in your place.

WEEK **ONE** · DAY **SIX**

THE ONLY WAY

There is nothing like heading home. If you have ever been away for a long time, you know there is nothing like driving back into your neighborhood, pulling onto your street and eventually parking in your own driveway. There is a peace that comes in knowing you are where you belong. That is what Jesus offers every person who turns to Him — a way home.

On the night before His death, Jesus told His disciples, *"I am the way, the truth, and the life. No one can come to the Father except through me,"* **(John 14.6 NLT)**. In this one simple sentence, Jesus made some bold claims. He said, *"I am ... the truth."* Not just that He knew the truth or pointed people to the truth, but that He was the truth of God embodied. All the promises of God and hopes of the people were once and for all wrapped up and fulfilled in Jesus. He said, *"I am ... the life."* Only Jesus gives life to the fullest here and eternal life in the hereafter.

He also claimed, *"I am the way."* The way where? The way back to God. Just as an on-ramp brings you back onto a highway, Jesus is the only way back to God and the path of life He has for you. You may ask, *"In a world of so many different religions, why is Jesus the only way?"* The simple answer is that there is no one like Jesus. He is the only one who fulfilled hundreds of ancient Jewish prophecies describing the coming Messiah. He is the only one who legitimately claimed to be God. Other religious leaders claimed to know God, but Jesus claimed to be God. Jesus is the only one who died for the sins of all people. No religious leader claimed to do such a thing. Jesus is the only one to defeat the grave. Check the graves of the other religious leaders, and you will find their bones, but Jesus' grave is empty.

Jesus is also the only one to offer eternal life in His name. Most religions are based on doing good works to earn eternal life, but Jesus offers life based on His finished work on the cross. Compared to everyone else, Jesus stands head and shoulders above the rest. Jesus is the only way to God.

Not only did Jesus claim to be the only way back to God, He also warned that other ways lead to destruction. *"You can enter God's Kingdom only through the narrow gate. The highway to hell is broad, and its gate is wide for the many who choose that way. But the gateway to life is very narrow and the road is difficult, and only a few ever find it,"* **(Matthew 7.13-14 NLT)**. Most people are traveling the *"wayward road"* that leads away from God. Jesus warned that road is like an eight-lane highway that ultimately leads to destruction.

The *"only way"* back home is a narrow way through Jesus alone, and only a few choose to walk that road. **(1 John 5.12 NLT)** makes it clear: *"Whoever has the Son has life; whoever does not have God's Son does not have life."*

THINK IT OUT

What did Jesus mean when He said, *"I am the way"*?

What do you think about the statement, *"Jesus is the only way to God"*?

Are you convinced that Jesus is the only way? If not, why not?

___

LIVE IT OUT

Review your Scripture memory verse for the week:

"For God so loved the world, that he gave his one and only Son, that whoever believes in him shall not perish but have eternal life."
(JOHN 3.16 NIV)

PRAY IT OUT

Take time to thank Jesus for making a way for you.

WEEK **ONE** · DAY **SEVEN**

HEADED HOME

Heading home is a choice. While Jesus made a way for you to be right with God, you still must respond to what He has done. How should you respond? Jesus made it very clear in His first recorded sermon. **(Mark 1.15 NIV)** says, *"The time has come," he said. "The kingdom of God has come near. Repent and believe the good news!"* In this short statement, Jesus proclaimed that the kingdom of God and the promised Messiah had come. Now people are called to respond in two ways.

First, Jesus said *"repent."* Repentance means to simply change your mind and change your direction. A repenting person is aware of his or her sin and is broken over it. **(Psalm 38.18 NLT)** says, *"But I confess my sins; I am deeply sorry for what I have done."*

Instead of blaming others, minimizing, or excusing, a repentant person is broken over the sin and willingly turns from it. Repentance also means that you see the direction you are going on that wayward road, and you make a conscious decision to turn off of it and leave your old lifestyle behind to follow the leadership of Jesus and obey Him.

You can't follow Jesus and keep going your way. Jesus calls us to be His disciples, walk as He walked and join Him in His mission. **(1 John 2.6 NIV)** says, *"Whoever claims to live in him must live as Jesus did."* Repentance means turning the corner and acknowledging Jesus as the forgiver and leader of your life.

Jesus also said we respond to all He has done by believing in Him. The Apostle Paul told a Philippian jailer, *"Believe in the Lord Jesus, and you will be saved,"* **(Acts 16.31 NIV)**. To *"believe in the Lord Jesus"* means to believe that Jesus is who He claimed to be and that He has done what He claimed to do. It means acknowledging Jesus as the Son of God, who died in your place, was buried and rose again in power.

Believing also means that you act on what you believe to be true. To believe in Jesus involves a decision to place your trust and hope in Him alone for your forgiveness and your eternity. No longer are you trusting in your own efforts, good works or religious practice to save you. You are trusting in Jesus alone and His work on the cross. **(Romans 10.9 ESV)** states, *"If you confess with your mouth that Jesus is Lord and believe in your heart that God raised him from the dead, you will be saved."*

THINK IT OUT

What does repentance mean?

What does it mean to believe in Jesus?

Have you decided to repent and believe in Jesus?

LIVE IT OUT

Review your Scripture memory verse for the week:

"For God so loved the world, that he gave his one and only Son, that whoever believes in him shall not perish but have eternal life."
(JOHN 3.16 NIV)

PRAY IT OUT

Take time to thank Jesus for giving you a heart to repent and believe the gospel.

WEEK **ONE**

FOR GROUP TIME

My "I Will" Statement:
As a result of what I have just studied, I will put this one thing into practice this week:

_____
_____
_____
_____
_____
_____
_____
_____
_____

JESUS AT THE CENTER

WEEK TWO

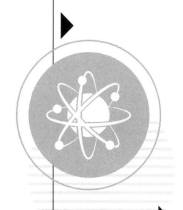

▶ **MEMORY VERSE**

"But seek first the kingdom of God and his righteousness, and all these things will be added to you."

(MATTHEW 6.33 ESV)

WEEK **TWO** · DAY **ONE**

EVERYTHING HAS A CENTER

What is at the center of your life? It's an important question to think about. Whatever is at the center is the most important part of you. Like the hub of a wheel, it is what drives you, what empowers you, what consumes you.

For some people, their career is the center of their life. Nothing is more important than climbing the ladder of success or accomplishing their goals. For others, it's a relationship. A boyfriend or girlfriend, a spouse or a child, maybe even a best friend consumes every waking thought and gives meaning to life. Whatever is at the center, is what you think about constantly and value the most.

Everyone has something at the center.

The smallest particles of matter have a center. Electrons perpetually encircle a center nucleus. Now think about the largest creations. Colossal planets in space also orbit a center. God created all things to revolve around a center, and God created you to have Jesus at the center of your life.

Following Jesus means making Him the center of your life — meaning everything else revolves around Jesus. This week we are going to look at what it means to make Jesus the center and how you can live with Him at the center of your life on a daily basis. As you do this, you find that Jesus Himself becomes the source of your hope, strength and joy.

THINK IT OUT

How do you respond to the statement, "Everyone has something at the center"?
Do you agree or disagree? Why?

_____
_____
_____
_____
_____
_____
_____
_____
_____
_____

What is the center and driving force in your life?

_____
_____
_____
_____
_____
_____
_____
_____
_____
_____
_____

LIVE IT OUT

Begin memorizing your Scripture memory verse for the week:

"But seek first the kingdom of God and his righteousness, and all these things will be added to you."
(MATTHEW 6.33 ESV)

Review your *"I Will"* statement for this week.

PRAY IT OUT

Ask God to show you anything that is taking His place as the center of your life.

WEEK **TWO** · DAY **TWO**

WHAT DOES IT MEAN TO MAKE JESUS THE CENTER OF MY LIFE?

Imagine over 2 million Jewish slaves wandering in the wilderness. For 400 years they were enslaved in Egypt, providing the hard labor force to support the luxurious lifestyle of its citizens. God had heard their cries and brought them out by His own power under the direction of Moses. Next, they were wandering, waiting on the Lord to bring them into the land He promised them. When the people settled in an area, God gave specific instructions on how to make camp. Certain tribes were to camp on the north and south, others on the east and west. The center of camp was reserved for the tabernacle — a portable structure where the people gathered to worship the Lord. God was at the center.

That is the way God wanted it then, and that is the way He wants it today. You were designed for the purpose of knowing Jesus Christ and making Him the center of your life. You may ask, *"What do you mean, make Jesus the center of my life?"* It means you acknowledge Jesus as the ultimate authority in your life and you voluntarily yield the control of your life to Him.

Underline that last statement. Let it sink in. For Jesus to be the center of your life, it means He is in control. You no longer desire to independently run your own life, but you surrender your whole self to Jesus and to following His lead.

Now your second question may be, *"Why would I do that?"* Don't we all want to be in control? As William Ernest Henley wrote in his poem, *"Invictus"*: *"I am the master of my fate, I am the captain of my soul."* Our wayward self always wants to control our own life, but following Jesus means that you give Him control. He calls the shots. The sign hanging on the door of your life reads: *"Now under new management."*

Why should you allow Jesus to be the center and leader of your life? First, Jesus created you and ultimately all things are under His rule — including you. **"And he is before all things, and in him all things hold together. ... He is the beginning, the firstborn from the dead, that in everything he might be preeminent," (Colossians 1.17-18 ESV)**. Second, Jesus controls everything. **(1 Timothy 6.15 JBP)** calls Jesus the *"blessed controller of all things."* Third, Jesus is faithful. **(2 Thessalonians 3.3 NLT)** says, *"But the Lord is faithful; He will strengthen you and guard you from the evil one."*

He created you, He controls everything and He is faithful — why wouldn't you want Jesus to be the center and controller of your life? It's clear that Jesus can do a better job of running your life than you can, so let Him lead you each day.

THINK IT OUT

What does it mean for Jesus to be the center of your life?

_____
_____
_____
_____
_____
_____
_____
_____
_____
_____
_____

Why is Jesus uniquely qualified to be the center of your life?

_____
_____
_____
_____
_____
_____
_____
_____
_____
_____

In what ways do you struggle to give Jesus control of your life?

_____
_____
_____
_____
_____
_____
_____
_____

LIVE IT OUT

Review your Scripture memory verse for the week:

"But seek first the kingdom of God and his righteousness, and all these things will be added to you."
(MATTHEW 6.33 ESV)

Review your *"I Will"* statement for this week.

PRAY IT OUT

Take time in prayer to voluntarily yield control of your life to Jesus.

WEEK **TWO** · DAY **THREE**

THE CENTER OF YOUR THOUGHTS

In May 1971, a Texas newspaper featured an article titled *"What They're Saying"* that quoted Frank Outlaw, president of the successful supermarket chain BI-LO:

"Watch your thoughts, they become words;
watch your words, they become actions;
watch your actions, they become habits;
watch your habits, they become character;
watch your character, for it becomes your destiny."

It all starts with your thoughts. Your thoughts drive your words, your actions, your habits, your character and ultimately, your destiny. So, if Jesus is going to be the center of your life, it starts with your thoughts. The Apostle Paul urged the new Christians in Rome to let God's Word change the way they thought. *"Don't copy the behavior and customs of this world, but let God transform you into a new person by changing the way you think. Then you will learn to know God's will for you, which is good and pleasing and perfect,"* **(Romans 12.2 NLT)**.

God changes you into a new person by first changing the way you think. Let's start there. What do you think about? What consumes your waking moments? When your mind rests and disengages from the immediate task at hand, where does it go? That is the place where Jesus wants to be most at home, in the forefront of your mind. To make Jesus center means that your thoughts run to Jesus and your desire is to please Him more than anything, **(2 Corinthians 5.9 ESV)**.

The author of Hebrews put it this way: *"Therefore, holy brothers and sisters, who share in the heavenly calling, fix your thoughts on Jesus, whom we acknowledge as our apostle and high priest,"* **(Hebrews 3.1 NIV)**. Jesus is the ultimate apostle (which means *"sent one"*). He was sent from heaven to earth to redeem you and show His grace toward you. He is also the ultimate *"high priest"* — the one who represents God to the people and the people to God.

We are told to *"fix our thoughts on Jesus."* In **(2 Corinthians 10.5 ESV)**, the Apostle Paul tells us to *"take every thought captive to obey Christ"*. We need to evaluate our thoughts. Capture them and see if they are pleasing to God. Every thought that doesn't please God has to go! One way you can do that is to read God's Word on a daily basis. As you read God's Word, He will speak to you and set your thoughts on Him.

The Apostle Paul wrote to the church in Philippi, *"And now, dear brothers and sisters, one final thing. Fix your thoughts on what is true, and honorable, and right, and pure, and lovely, and admirable. Think about things that are excellent and worthy of praise. Keep putting into practice all you learned and received from me — everything you heard from me and saw me doing. Then the God of peace will be with you,"* **(Philippians 4.8-9 NLT)**. I love these verses because they are so practical. In effect, Paul is saying *"garbage in, garbage out."* If you put godless things in your mind, you will never experience transformation. However, if you set your mind on God's Word and all that is true, honorable, right, pure, lovely and admirable — if you set your mind on these things and practice them, then you will experience God's peace.

THINK IT OUT

Why is it important to set your thoughts on Jesus?

___

What do you set your thoughts on throughout the day?

___

What steps can you take to keep garbage out of your thought life?

_____
_____
_____
_____
_____
_____
_____
_____
_____

LIVE IT OUT

Review your Scripture memory verse for the week:

"But seek first the kingdom of God and his righteousness, and all these things will be added to you."
(MATTHEW 6.33 ESV)

Review your *"I Will"* statement for this week.

PRAY IT OUT

Ask God to reveal anything in you that is not pleasing to Him.

WEEK **TWO** · DAY **FOUR**

THE CENTER OF YOUR HEART

Among the ruins of ancient Rome sits a small dungeon still intact. In its prime, it was nothing more than a dark, circular, underground hole with plastered walls and a single opening on top where they lowered prisoners into confinement. It was a lonely place — a desperate place. Today you can tour it, going down into the belly of the cell. Against the wall is a stone pillar with an inscription indicating that the Apostles Paul and Peter were held there. It was probably there that Paul wrote these words:

> " [For my determined purpose is] that I may know Him [that I may progressively become more deeply and intimately acquainted with Him, perceiving and recognizing and understanding the wonders of His Person more strongly and more clearly], and that I may in that same way come to know the power outflowing from His resurrection [[a]which it exerts over believers], and that I may so share His sufferings as to be continually transformed [in spirit into His likeness even] to His death, [in the hope]."
>
> **(Philippians 3.10 AMPC)**

Read those words again. Think about each line. Paul's *"determined purpose"* was simply to know Jesus. His singular passion, his heart cry, his driving force was to know Jesus deeply and personally. He wanted to grasp the *"wonders of His Person"* — this is worship. He wanted to know experientially the resurrection power of Jesus Christ working through his life. Even in his suffering, Paul wanted to be shaped into the likeness of Jesus. Jesus was at the center of Paul's life.

Just a few verses earlier Paul said that everything else he had pursued in life was a waste. At one point, Paul was on the fast track to fame and power. He was a rising star in his field, surpassing all the rest. He had all that this world says is important — wealth, prestige, success, respect. But when he met Jesus, nothing else mattered. Nothing could compare to knowing and following Jesus.

The same is true today. Pursuing anything other than Jesus with your one single life is simply a waste of time. One hundred years from now nothing else will have lasted and nothing else will matter. The famous evangelist Billy Graham once said, *"The ultimate experience in life is knowing Jesus."*

This is the great promise of Jesus: if you make it your determined purpose to know and follow Him, He will show Himself to you. In **(John 15.4-5 ESV)** Jesus said, *"Abide in me, and I in you. As the branch cannot bear fruit by itself, unless it abides in the vine, neither can you, unless you abide in me. I am the vine; you are the branches. Whoever abides in me and I in him, he it is that bears much fruit, for apart from me you can do nothing."* To abide means to make yourself at home. So to abide in Jesus means to draw close to Him, to seek to know Him more deeply. Only when we abide in Jesus can we really be used by Him to do great things.

What's your determined purpose? What drives you and defines you? That one thing is what you worship, and what you worship sits at the center of your heart. *How can you know?* Follow the trail of your time, your money and your desires, and they will lead you to what has your heart.

THINK IT OUT

What does it mean to make knowing Jesus your determined purpose?

_____
_____
_____
_____
_____
_____
_____
_____
_____
_____
_____
_____
_____

Why is pursuing anything else a waste of time?

___

When you follow the trail of your time, money and passion where does it lead?

___

LIVE IT OUT

Review your Scripture memory verse for the week:

"But seek first the kingdom of God and his righteousness, and all these things will be added to you."
(MATTHEW 6.33 ESV)

Review your *"I Will"* statement for this week.

PRAY IT OUT

Ask God to show you your determined purpose, and surrender that purpose to Jesus.

WEEK **TWO** · DAY **FIVE**

THE CENTER OF YOUR PRIORITIES

Think about your priorities before you came to Christ. Your list for the day probably included things to do for your family, things to do for work and a few fun things just for yourself. All in all, your life was mostly about what was important to you.

But the follower of Jesus has a different set of priorities. While many of those other things are still on the list, what tops the list is pleasing Jesus and doing what is important to Him. Jesus Himself is the perfect model for us. Jesus said, *"I seek not to please myself but him who sent me,"* **(John 5.30 NIV)**.

And again, *"The one who sent me is with me; he has not left me alone, for I always do what pleases him,"* **(John 8.29 NIV)**.

Jesus always had His Father's desires as His first priority. Now, just as Jesus made His priorities match His Father's priorities, we are called to do the same thing. Our priorities need to match the priorities of Jesus. **(2 Corinthians 5.15 NLT)** says *"He died for everyone so that those who receive his new life will no longer live for themselves. Instead, they will live for Christ, who died and was raised for them."* This is the normal Christian life — making Jesus' life and mission our top priority. No longer do we live for ourselves; we live for Christ. No longer do we live to just please ourselves; we live to please King Jesus.

What do you think were some of Jesus' priorities? Worship was a priority. Jesus always exalted the Father as the source of every good thing. In **(John 17.7 ESV)** Jesus tells His Father, *"Now they know that everything that you have given me is from you."* Jesus never took credit for the good things in His life; He always acknowledged and worshiped His Father.

Prayer was a priority for Jesus. More than seventy times the Gospels record Jesus either speaking about or modeling prayer. Obedience was a priority for Jesus. Jesus always gave Himself to His Father's kingdom agenda. Dependence on the Spirit, reliance on God's Word, sharing the gospel and cultivating healthy relationships — all these things were priorities for Jesus. Now, if these were Jesus' priorities, don't you think they should be ours too?

Halfway through Jesus' ministry He sat down on a hillside and preached a message that is now called the Sermon on the Mount. Buried in that sermon, He makes this statement: *"But seek first the kingdom of God and his righteousness, and all these things will be added to you,"* **(Matthew 6.33 ESV)**. Many times we are afraid that if we make Jesus' priorities our own, we will miss out on a lot of things. But Jesus promised that if we live for Him rather than ourselves and if we put Him and His priorities first in our lives, then He will give us the things that really matter. The things that don't matter won't matter anymore.

THINK IT OUT

What are some of Jesus' priorities?

How do your priorities match up against Jesus' priorities?

LIVE IT OUT

Review your Scripture memory verse for the week:

"But seek first the kingdom of God and his righteousness, and all these things will be added to you."
(MATTHEW 6.33 ESV)

Review your *"I Will"* statement for this week.

PRAY IT OUT

Ask God to help you make adjustments to make Jesus' priorities your own.

WEEK **TWO** · DAY **SIX**

STEPPING DOWN

A wise person finds balance to life. Usually when we think of balance, we picture our life like a scale. Balance is found in dividing our time, resources and energy evenly among all the demands of our life. Everything is segmented; everybody gets their fair share.

Unfortunately, life just doesn't work that way. Work demands more than its share, family needs more of you and then, there are eternal priorities. No one ever seems to get enough, and you are left worn out.

Now, think of a plate spinning on a stick. It spins without falling because the stick is placed perfectly in the center and the whole plate spins around that center point. When Jesus is at the center of your life, He will lead you and empower you to live for Him in every area of your life — where you live, learn, work and play.

So how do you live with Jesus in the center of your life? Lean in close and listen to the Apostle Paul's words: *"Do not let any part of your body become an instrument of evil to serve sin. Instead, give yourselves completely to God, for you were dead, but now you have new life,"* **(Romans 6.13 NLT)**.

Underline the words *"give yourselves completely to God."* Other versions put the same thought in different words: *"yield yourself to God," "offer yourselves to God," "present yourselves to God," "put yourself in God's hands," "put yourself at God's disposal."* The key to living with Jesus in the center of your life is surrendering control to Him day by day and moment by moment.

Imagine a huge throne. It's the center of all power and control. This is the throne of your life, and you sit on that throne, living for yourself and following your own plans. Now Jesus steps into the room and wants to sit on the throne of your life. He wants to be in control. Living with Jesus at the center means you step down from that throne of control and allow Jesus to take His rightful place in your life.

Now picture you are driving a car. You are setting the course and calling the shots, but then Jesus steps into the car and wants to drive. Living with Jesus in the center means allowing Jesus to sit behind the wheel of your life and lead you.

Whether you envision a throne or a car, Jesus wants to lead your life. He wants to be the center of your life — around which everything revolves. This is not just a one-time experience; it's a daily practice.

How can you do this? Commit to live your life for Him one day at a time. You can't change your past. It's done. You can't change your future. That is in God's hands. You can only live in this moment. So live one day at a time, and each day choose to let Jesus lead your life.

That may start in the mornings with prayer and studying your Bible. Before the day starts, you slip to your knees and pray, "Jesus, today I want you to be the center of my life around which everything revolves. I want to please you and live for you. I yield myself to you today. Please fill me with your Spirit to live for you today." That's a great way to start the day!

But be warned: Sometime during the day, you may take the throne or grab the wheel again. Anger will surge, temptation will win, selfishness will rise up, and you will sin against God. When you do, confess it quickly to God. **(1 John 1.9 NIV)** says, *"If we confess our sins, he is faithful and just and will forgive us our sins and purify us from all unrighteousness."* Confess your sin and then yield yourself once again to Him. *"Lord, I want you to fill me and use me today. I'm yielding the control of my life to you!"*

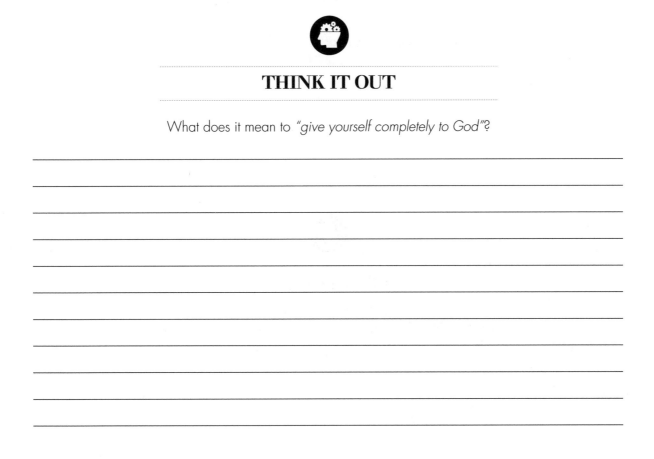

THINK IT OUT

What does it mean to *"give yourself completely to God"*?

_____
_____
_____
_____
_____
_____
_____
_____
_____
_____

In what areas do you need to step down from control and yield to God?

_____
_____
_____
_____
_____
_____
_____
_____
_____

LIVE IT OUT

Review your Scripture memory verse for the week:

"But seek first the kingdom of God and his righteousness, and all these things will be added to you."
(MATTHEW 6.33 ESV)

Review your *"I Will"* statement for this week.

PRAY IT OUT

Surrender control of your life today and ask Jesus to lead you.

WEEK **TWO** · DAY **SEVEN**

SURRENDERING TO THE SPIRIT

Living with Jesus at the center is not easy. In fact, it's a battle. Your old wayward, sinful self will fight every step along the way, but Jesus made a provision for you to enable you to yield to Him and follow Him completely. On the night before His death, Jesus spoke to His disciples. *"If you love me, you will keep my commandments. And I will ask the Father, and he will give you another Helper, to be with you forever, even the Spirit of truth, whom the world cannot receive, because it neither sees him nor knows him. You know him, for he dwells with you and will be in you,"* **(John 14.15-17 ESV)**.

Jesus promised that He would send you a Helper, the Holy Spirit. Who is the Holy Spirit? For starters, the Holy Spirit is a person. He is not a force or power. He is the third person of the Trinity. God exists in three persons: the Father, the Son and the Holy Spirit. Here Jesus refers to the Holy Spirit as your *"Helper."* The word literally means advocate, encourager or one who comes alongside to help you. The Holy Spirit is the one Jesus sent to come alongside you to help you.

You may ask, *"How does the Holy Spirit help me?"* Jesus gives us several ways in this passage: 1) He comforts you. The word "helper" can also be translated "comforter." When you are discouraged, the Spirit comforts your heart. 2) He stays with you. Jesus said He is with you forever. He will never leave or abandon you. 3) He teaches you truth, showing you right from wrong and how to please God. 4) He empowers you to live boldly for Jesus. **(Acts 1.8 NIV)** says, *"But you will receive power when the Holy Spirit comes on you; and you will be my witnesses."* 5) He changes you from the inside out, filling you with *"love, joy, peace, patience, kindness, goodness, faithfulness, gentleness and self-control,"* **(Galatians 5.22-23 ESV)**.

Relying solely on your own strength, you cannot live the Christian life, but when you are filled with and controlled by the Spirit, you can! The Apostle Paul gave this command: *"be filled with the Holy Spirit,"* **(Ephesians 5.18 NLT)**. How can you be filled with the Spirit? You can begin by believing in Jesus. The Spirit comes into your life at the moment of your salvation. **(Ephesians 1.13 NLT)** says, *"And when you believed in Christ, he identified you as his own by giving you the Holy Spirit, whom he promised long ago."* If you are a Christ follower, then you have the Holy Spirit.

Now you have to walk with Him, following His promptings and heeding His warnings. When you do something the Spirit is warning you not to do, you grieve the Spirit, **(Ephesians 4.30 ESV)**. When you don't do something the Spirit is prompting you to do, you quench the Spirit, **(1 Thessalonians 5.19 ESV)**. But when you do what the Spirit is leading you to do, you are walking in the Spirit, **(Galatians 5.25 ESV)**. Then you are *"filled with the Holy Spirit,"* **(Ephesians 5.18 ESV)**, and the power of the Spirit is released in your life!

THINK IT OUT

Who is the Holy Spirit?

_____
_____
_____
_____
_____
_____

What does the Holy Spirit do for you?

_____
_____
_____
_____
_____
_____

In what areas do you sense you are not walking in step with the Spirit?

_____
_____
_____
_____
_____
_____

LIVE IT OUT

Review your Scripture memory verse for the week:

"But seek first the kingdom of God and his righteousness, and all these things will be added to you."
(MATTHEW 6.33 ESV)

Review your *"I Will"* statement for this week.

PRAY IT OUT

Ask the Holy Spirit to fill you and help you to trust and follow Jesus.

FOR GROUP TIME
My *"I Will"* Statement:
As a result of what I have just studied, I will put this one thing into practice this week:

_____
_____
_____
_____
_____
_____
_____
_____
_____

LISTENING TO
GOD

WEEK THREE

MEMORY VERSE

"My sheep listen to my voice; I know them, and they follow me."

(JOHN 10.27 NIV)

WEEK **THREE** · DAY **ONE**

HEARING GOD'S VOICE

You were created to know God in a deep and personal way. He never intended for your relationship with Him to be distant, formal or mechanical. He knows you. He has a plan for you that is beautiful, adventurous and significant. And most of all, He created you to have fellowship with Him.

The Apostle Paul wrote to the church in Corinth, *"God is faithful, who has called you into fellowship with his Son, Jesus Christ our Lord,"* **(1 Corinthians 1.9 NIV)**. The word *"fellowship"* means to share life together. Think about it: Jesus always lived in close, loving fellowship with His Father. He listened to His Father and obeyed Him completely.

On one occasion Jesus said, *"For the Father loves the Son and shows him all he does,"* **(John 5.20 NIV)**. Another time Jesus told His followers, *"I have loved you even as the Father has loved me. Remain in my love. When you obey my commandments, you remain in my love, just as I obey my Father's commandments and remain in his love,"* **(John 15.9-10 NLT)**.

From eternity past, Jesus enjoyed unbroken love and fellowship with the Father because He was always obedient to His Father. Now He invites you into that fellowship. When you came to Christ, you stepped into fellowship with Jesus and with the Father — the same fellowship that Jesus enjoyed with the Father from the beginning of time.

Jesus told His disciples, *"When I am raised to life again, you will know that I am in my Father, and you are in me, and I am in you,"* **(John 14.20 NLT)**. What an amazing thought!

Now, the basis for any fellowship is communication. God wants you to hear His voice and follow Him. You may be thinking, *"Does God really speak today?"* Absolutely! He has always spoken to His people. God spoke to Noah about how to build a boat. God spoke to Joshua and told him to march around Jericho. God spoke to David and gave plans for the temple. God spoke to Daniel with prophecies of the future. God spoke to Elijah and brought fire down from heaven. God spoke to Moses face to face, as one friend to another.

(Psalm 50.3 NIV) says, *"Our God comes and will not be silent."* The question is not, *"Does God still speak?"* The question is, *"Are you listening?"*

Do you know how to listen to God? All through the Scriptures we are directed to listen to God's voice and obey Him. Consider the following verses:

- *"...love the LORD your God, listen to his voice, and hold fast to him..."* **(Deuteronomy 30.20 NIV)**.

- *"I listen carefully to what God the LORD is saying, for he speaks peace to his faithful people..."* **(Psalm 85.8 NLT)**.

- *"...Speak, for your servant is listening,"* **(1 Samuel 3.10 NIV)**.

- *"He who has ears to hear, let him hear,"* **(Matthew 11.15 ESV)**.

- *"Today, if you hear his voice, do not harden your hearts as you did in the rebellion,"* **(Hebrews 3.15 NIV)**.

THINK IT OUT

Do you think God still speaks today? Why or why not?

___
___
___
___
___
___
___
___
___
___

Has there been a time when you believe you heard from God? If so, when?

_____
_____
_____
_____
_____
_____
_____
_____
_____
_____

LIVE IT OUT

Begin memorizing your Scripture memory verse for the week:

"My sheep listen to my voice; I know them, and they follow me."
(JOHN 10.27 NIV)

Review your *"I Will"* statement for this week.

PRAY IT OUT

Ask God to speak to you as you read His Word. Thank Him for preserving His Word so you can read it and know Him.

WEEK **THREE** · DAY **TWO**

HOW TO LISTEN TO GOD

The primary way God speaks to us today is through His Word, the Bible. In **(2 Timothy 3.16-17 NLT)** the Apostle Paul wrote: *"All Scripture is inspired by God and is useful to teach us what is true and to make us realize what is wrong in our lives. It corrects us when we are wrong and teaches us to do what is right. God uses it to prepare and equip his people to do every good work."*

The words *"inspired by God"* literally mean *"God breathed."* God spoke His Word through the Holy Spirit to chosen men who wrote it down for us to read, **(2 Peter 1.21 ESV)**. It's God's Word that teaches us right from wrong. It's God's Word that corrects us when we get off track and shows us how to live in a way that pleases God. It's called the *"word of life,"* **(Philippians 2.16 ESV)**. It is *"living and active,"* **(Hebrews 4.12 ESV)**. It *"stands forever,"* **(Isaiah 40.8 NLT)**.

The Bible is the most unique book ever written. It was written over 1,500 years by more than 40 human authors in three different languages. These authors came from various cultures and walks of life. Over and over its historical accuracy has been confirmed, and its prophecies have proved true and continue to affirm its reliability. No other book has been more scrutinized and attacked than the Bible, and yet God preserved it for you today.

(Psalm 19.7-11 NLT) describes the wonder of God's Word for us: *"The instructions of the LORD are perfect, reviving the soul. The decrees of the LORD are trustworthy, making wise the simple. The commandments of the LORD are right, bringing joy to the heart. The commands of the LORD are clear, giving insight for living. Reverence for the LORD is pure, lasting forever. The laws of the LORD are true; each one is fair. They are more desirable than gold, even the finest gold. They are sweeter than honey, even honey dripping from the comb. They are a warning to your servant, a great reward for those who obey them."*

God wrote a book, and through His Word He communicates who He is, what He has done and how we can know Him personally. Listening to God begins with listening to His Word.

Jesus is a great example for us to follow. Jesus saturated His life with God's Word. As a young man Jesus would have memorized most of the first five books of the Old Testament. Throughout His ministry He quoted eighty times from more than seventy different Old Testament passages. Often Jesus rebuked the religious leaders because they didn't know the Scriptures, **(Matthew 21.16, 22.29, 31 ESV)**. Jesus was devoted to God's Word, and you should be too.

In order to learn how to listen to God, we are going to create an acrostic to show us practical ways to **"l.i.s.t.e.n."** to God through reading His Word. Today we are going to look at the first two letters.

L stands for **look at a passage from God's Word**. Listening begins with looking into God's Word. If God speaks primarily through His Word, then you need to read God's Word to hear from Him. Make it a habit to read God's Word every day. Before you begin reading each day, stop and pray. Ask God to open your eyes to see Him and open your ears to hear His voice. Pray, *"Speak Lord, I'm listening to you."*

I stands for **identify what stands out**. As you read, be sensitive to what the Spirit of God is pointing out for you to notice. Oftentimes, a word or phrase will stand out. Sometimes, the Spirit will point out a teaching that directly applies to you. Don't read casually for content; read actively, looking for what God has for you that day. When verses stand out, underline or highlight them in your Bible.

THINK IT OUT

What is so unique about the Bible?

What would keep you from reading God's Word daily?

___

LIVE IT OUT

Review your memory verse for the week:

"My sheep listen to my voice; I know them, and they follow me."
(JOHN 10.27 NIV)

Review your *"I Will"* statement for this week.

PRAY IT OUT

Ask God to speak to you as you read His Word.
Thank Him for preserving His Word so you can read it and know Him.

WEEK **THREE** • DAY **THREE**

DIVING DEEPER

God's Word is the primary way God speaks to you. As you read His Word, your goal should not be to casually read simply for content as you would a history book. Nor should you read God's Word for entertainment as you would a novel. You read God's Word to know Him more deeply and personally, just as you would a love letter.

God's Word is His love letter to you. Your goal should never be merely to get through the daily reading assignment. Many people read a chapter and check that box on their *"to-do list,"* but they never hear God's voice. The goal isn't to master the reading assignment; it is to meet with the Master. If you only read a few verses and yet you hear God's voice, then that is all you really need for that day. Remember that you were created for fellowship with Jesus, so read listening for His voice.

Now that you are reading God's Word and identifying key verses or passages that the Spirit of God points out for you, it's time to dive deeper. So, let's take a look at the next two letters of our **"l.i.s.t.e.n."** acrostic.

S stands for **study God's truth**. Now that you are focused on a few passages, study them. Look at them closely. Picture what is happening. Write down your observations. Ask yourself some key questions as you study the passages.

- Is there an attitude mentioned that I need to change?
- Is there a command here that I need to follow?
- Is there a truth here that I need to understand?
- Is there a sin mentioned that I need to confess or avoid?

As you study, ask God to show you what He wants you to learn from this Scripture.

T stands for **think about how this applies to your life.** Once you have a clear picture of the meaning, ponder it in your heart. Think deeply about how these truths apply to your life. This is what the Bible calls meditation.

Many people think of meditation as emptying your mind and thinking of pleasant things. But biblical meditation is focusing on God's Word and asking God to apply it to your life. **(Psalm 119.15 NIV)** says, *"I meditate on your precepts and consider your ways."*

God told Joshua, *"Study this Book of Instruction continually. Meditate on it day and night so you will be sure to obey everything written in it. Only then will you prosper and succeed in all you do,"* **(Joshua 1.8 NLT)**. When you study God's Word and meditate on how it applies to your life, you are moving God's Word from your head to your heart.

THINK IT OUT

What are some questions you can ask to help you study God's Word?

_____
_____
_____
_____
_____
_____
_____
_____
_____
_____
_____
_____
_____
_____
_____
_____

What is biblical meditation? Why is it important?

___

LIVE IT OUT

Review your Scripture memory verse for the week:

"My sheep listen to my voice; I know them, and they follow me."
(JOHN 10.27 NIV)

Review your *"I Will"* statement for this week.

PRAY IT OUT

Ask God to speak to you as you read His Word. Ask Him to reveal truth so you can understand and apply His Word to your life.

WEEK **THREE** · DAY **FOUR**

GETTING IT DOWN

Communication is not a one-way street. For a couple to truly communicate, they need to have a conversation — not just a monologue. Both must be engaged in listening and talking. The same is true in your relationship with God.

God wants to speak to you, but He also wants you to pour out your heart to Him. God is speaking, and you are learning to listen to His voice by reading God's Word, identifying key passages, studying them and meditating on how they apply to your life. These next two steps will help you get the most out of what God is speaking into your life.

E stands for **engage with God in prayer**. After you hear from God through His Word and you study it and meditate on how it applies to your life, then pray about that topic. Simply praying the Scripture back to God in your own words can be very powerful. Ask God to make the truth real in your life. If there is sin to confess, then confess it to Him quickly and receive His promised forgiveness, **(1 John 1.9 ESV)**. Now you and Jesus are engaged in a conversation that is meaningful and transforming.

N stands for **note what God says and what you pray in a journal**. It is important to write down what God says for several reasons:

> 1) It helps you remember what God has spoken in your life. If God convicts you to take some action, writing it down helps you remember to be obedient to do it. If God gives you a great promise or words of encouragement, writing it down helps you remember what He said.

> 2) Writing down your conversations with God encourages you over the years. When you can look back at dark seasons in your life and see how God spoke, it encourages you that He is faithful and will see you through your current challenges.

3) Writing down your conversations with God helps you pass on great promises and experiences to your children and others. Over the years, great men and women of faith have participated in spiritual journaling as a daily discipline for knowing God better.

Here are some practical tips as you begin to journal:
1) Date the page at the top so you will remember when God spoke to you.
2) Write down the key passage and any insights God gives you.
3) Record how the passage applies to your life. You may even want to personalize it, re-writing it with your name in it as if Jesus was speaking this directly to you.
4) Write down your personal prayer. Write as if you are writing a letter to Jesus.
5) Summarize what God spoke to you in a short title and write that at the top of the page.

I encourage you to keep these things physically or electronically so you can refer to them later. Another way you can *"note what God has said"* is to make a mental note by memorizing key passages that stand out to you. **(Psalm 119.11 NLT)** says, *"I have hidden your word in my heart, that I might not sin against you."*

(Deuteronomy 11.18 ESV) says, *"You shall therefore lay up these words of mine in your heart and in your soul."* As you read, study, meditate and memorize God's Word, you are hiding it in your heart and soul.

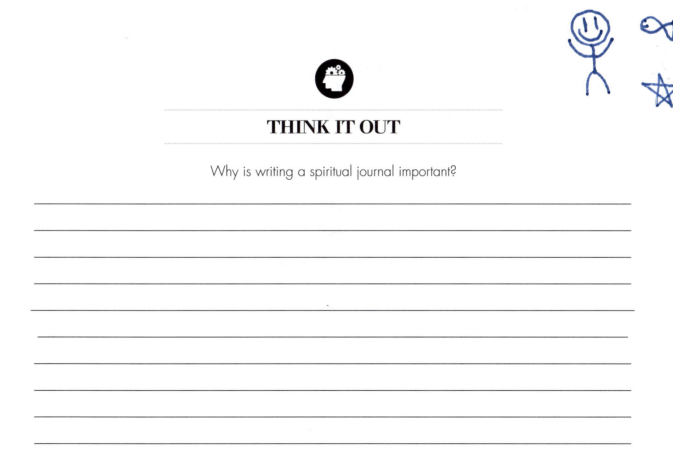

THINK IT OUT

Why is writing a spiritual journal important?

_____
_____
_____
_____
_____
_____
_____
_____
_____

What are some steps you need to take to record what God is speaking to you?

_____
_____
_____
_____
_____
_____
_____
_____
_____

LIVE IT OUT

Review your Scripture memory verse for the week:

"My sheep listen to my voice; I know them, and they follow me."
(JOHN 10.27 NIV)

Review your *"I Will"* statement for this week.

PRAY IT OUT

Ask God to speak to you as you read His Word. Ask Him to help you live out the things He has shown you today.

WEEK **THREE** · DAY **FIVE**

THE IMPORTANCE OF TIME WITH GOD

Imagine you are invited to the Oval Office to meet the President of the United States. Your heart begins to race with excitement. When will it happen? What should you do? How will you respond? What will the president say? If that meeting was actually going to happen, you can rest assured there would be a plan.

The same is true in your relationship with God. Meeting with God is far more important than meeting with the president, and it requires a plan.

Before we dive into the practical side, let me first say that investing time alone with God should be motivated by a deep desire to know Jesus more personally and intimately. If your determined purpose is to know Jesus, then you should be determined to meet with Him. Your time with God should never be out of mere duty or legalism. God's not looking for your mechanical worship; He's looking for true worshipers who approach Him openly and honestly, **(John 4.23 ESV)**. He wants your heart.

With that in mind, here are some things you can do to maximize your time alone with God:

Pick a time. It's important to choose a time when you can meet with God on a consistent basis. For many people, this time is first thing in the morning. The prophet Isaiah said, *"He wakens me morning by morning, wakens my ear to listen like one being instructed,"* **(Isaiah 50.4 NIV)**. Jesus Himself got up early to spend time with His Father. *"Very early in the morning, while it was still dark, Jesus got up, left the house, and went off to a solitary place, where he prayed,"* **(Mark 1.35 NIV)**. Usually the morning is best because you can hear from God at the start of your day. Also, you are fresh in the morning and disengaged from the rush of your daily schedule. While the morning may be preferred, the important thing is that you pick a time that works for you and your schedule.

Pick a place. You want to choose a place where you will not be distracted. Jesus went to a *"solitary place."* The word in Greek is *eremos*, and it means *"lonely or deserted."* Still today, just north of the Sea of Galilee, there is a cave that some call Eremos Cave where Jesus could have spent time alone with the Father, uninterrupted by the demands of the day. You need a place like that — a place away from people, your phone and your computer — where you can be still and worship God.

Pick your tools. Just like a carpenter goes to work with the right tools, you need the right tools to meet with God. Choose a Bible you can read and mark up. Choose a journal or device for taking notes. Choose a daily reading plan. While devotional books may be helpful, they can't compare to just hearing from Jesus directly through His Word. Make sure you spend your time following the **l.i.s.t.e.n.** plan as you read God's Word. When you do, you will spend rich and meaningful time in God's presence.

Pick the right mindset. Meeting with Jesus is an incredible privilege, so go into your time with the Lord with an attitude of expectation. Ask God to speak to you. Read and listen with attentive eagerness. Be ready to receive from Him what He wants to say to you and obey Him completely.

THINK IT OUT

What place is best for you to meet with God?

_____
_____
_____
_____
_____
_____
_____
_____
_____

What time works best for your schedule?

_____
_____
_____
_____
_____
_____
_____
_____
_____

What would keep you from meeting with God daily?

_____
_____
_____
_____
_____
_____
_____

LIVE IT OUT

Review your Scripture memory verse for the week:

"My sheep listen to my voice; I know them, and they follow me."
(JOHN 10.27 NIV))

Review your *"I Will"* statement for this week.

PRAY IT OUT

Ask God to give you the determination to meet with Him daily.

WEEK **THREE** · DAY **SIX**

LISTENING TO THE SPIRIT

God has given you everything you need to walk with Him. He put His hand on you, His Word before you, His people around you and His Spirit within you. And there are times when God will speak to you clearly by His Spirit. It is the Holy Spirit who reveals truth to you **(John 14.16-17 ESV)**, points you to Christ **(John 15.26 ESV)**, convicts you of your sin **(John 16.8-11 ESV)** and draws you to Jesus **(John 6.44 ESV)**.

From the very beginning, the Spirit of God was at work bringing you to the place of forgiveness in Christ and new life. Therefore, that same Spirit will be at work, leading you to fulfill God's plan for your life. He is your *"helper,"* **(John 14.16 ESV)**. According to God's Word, we are to live controlled by the Spirit **(Romans 8.5-8 ESV)**, be filled with the Spirit **(Ephesians 5.18-19 ESV)**, walk in the Spirit **(Galatians 5.16 ESV)** and keep in step with the Spirit **(Galatians 5.25 ESV)**. We are even told to listen to the Spirit **(Revelation 2.7 ESV)** and be led by the Spirit **(Romans 8.14 ESV)**. In fact, all we do should be motivated and directed by the Spirit. We are to pray in the Spirit **(Ephesians 6.18 ESV)**, sing in the Spirit **(Ephesians 5.19 ESV)** and love in the power of the Spirit **(Romans 5.5 ESV)**.

How do you listen to the Holy Spirit? The Spirit most often speaks to us in five ways:

1) **He speaks through God's Word.** Because God's Word was written by the Holy Spirit **(2 Peter 1.21 ESV)**, and is called the *"sword of the Spirit,"* **(Ephesians 6.17 ESV)**, it is the Holy Spirit who leads us through the Scriptures to open our minds to God's truth, **(John 15.26, 17.17 ESV)**.

2) **He speaks to our spirit.** Sometimes the Spirit will speak to us directly. **(Romans 8.16 NIV)** says, *"The Spirit himself testifies with our spirit that we are God's children."* Many times in Scripture, God spoke to His people through the prompting of His Spirit. At times, the Spirit may prompt you to do something or say something. Other times, the Spirit may warn you not to move forward or convict you of your sin.

3) **He speaks through circumstances.** At times, God's Spirit will lead through circumstances that can only be explained by His supernatural intervention, **(Acts 16.7 ESV)**.

4) **He speaks through other believers.** Paul wrote to the Thessalonians, *"...when you received the word of God, which you heard from us, you accepted it not as the word of men but as what it really is, the word of God,"* **(1 Thessalonians 2.13 ESV)**.

5) **He speaks through dreams.** Many times the Spirit of God spoke to His people through dreams. God spoke to Daniel, Peter, Joseph and many others through dreams, **(Job 33.14-17 ESV)**.

So, how can you discern whether or not what you are receiving is actually from the Spirit? The answer is simple; test everything to be sure it comes from God. **(1 Thessalonians 5.19-22 NIV)** warns us, *"Do not quench the Spirit. Do not treat prophecies with contempt but test them all; hold on to what is good, reject every kind of evil."* Again in **(1 John 4.1 ESV)** we read, *"Beloved, do not believe every spirit, but test the spirits to see whether they are from God, for many false prophets have gone out into the world."*

If the Spirit is speaking, He will always meet this threefold test:

1) **Does this glorify Jesus?** Jesus said, *"When the Spirit of truth comes, he will guide you into all truth. He will not speak on his own but will tell you what he has heard. He will tell you about the future. He will bring me glory by telling you whatever he receives from me,"* **(John 16.13-14 NLT)**.
2) **Is this in agreement with God's Word?** As I have said, the Holy Spirit is the author of Scripture and He will never contradict God's Word.
3) **Is this consistent with God's character?** God's Spirit will never lead in any way that is inconsistent with God's love, mercy, kindness, grace and justice that we see most clearly in Jesus.

THINK IT OUT

What are the ways the Spirit of God speaks to you?

_____
_____
_____
_____
_____
_____
_____
_____
_____

Have you ever experienced the Spirit speaking to you?

_____
_____
_____
_____
_____

How can you test to see if what you are receiving is from the Spirit?

_____
_____
_____
_____
_____
_____

LIVE IT OUT

Review your Scripture memory verse for the week:

"My sheep listen to my voice; I know them, and they follow me."
(JOHN 10.27 NIV)

Review your *"I Will"* statement for this week.

PRAY IT OUT

Ask God to lead you today by His Spirit.

WEEK **THREE** · DAY **SEVEN**

DON'T JUST LISTEN

All week we have been talking about listening to God. And as important as that is, listening is not enough. God isn't just looking for listeners; He's looking for people who listen to His voice and act on what they hear.

Jesus said, *"My sheep listen to my voice; I know them, and they follow me,"* **(John 10.27 NIV)**. Jesus wants listeners and followers. To listen to God and never act on what you hear would be the ultimate act of disobedience. Imagine a parent telling a child something important to do. The child makes eye contact, hears every word, but then refuses to do it. That is how God sees us when we listen but don't act.

James warned us not to fall into the *"listening only"* trap: **"But don't just listen to God's word. You must do what it says. Otherwise, you are only fooling yourselves. For if you listen to the word and don't obey, it is like glancing at your face in a mirror. You see yourself, walk away, and forget what you look like. But if you look carefully into the perfect law that sets you free, and if you do what it says and don't forget what you heard, then God will bless you for doing it,"** **(James 1.22-25 NLT)**.

According to James, when we listen but don't act, we are just deceiving ourselves. We think we are pleasing God simply because we listen, when in fact we are disobeying Him. There are many people who sit in church or read their Bibles, but have no intention of living out what Jesus is calling them to do. Soon their hearts are hard toward God. They are religious but rebellious. **(Hebrews 3.15 NIV)** warns us, *"Today if you hear his voice, do not harden your hearts as you did in the rebellion."*

There is an old saying: *"The same sun that melts the wax hardens the clay."* God speaks to us through His Word, and if our hearts are ready and eager to obey, that Word melts our hearts and makes us pliable and useful to God. He can shape us into His image and transform us from the inside out. But if our hearts are stubborn and rebellious, refusing to do what He has said, that same Word hardens our hearts. Our hard hearts keep us from knowing God or being used by Him. James is saying, *"Don't be rebellious toward God and harden your heart; listen and do what He says."*

THINK IT OUT

Why is doing what God says so important?

_____
_____
_____
_____
_____
_____
_____

Share a time when you hardened your heart toward God.

_____
_____
_____
_____
_____
_____
_____
_____
_____

LIVE IT OUT

Review your Scripture memory verse for the week:

"My sheep listen to my voice; I know them, and they follow me."
(JOHN 10.27 NIV)

Review your *"I Will"* statement for this week.

PRAY IT OUT

Ask God to keep your heart soft and pliable, ready to obey Him.

FOR GROUP TIME
My "I Will" Statement:
As a result of what I have just studied, I will put this one thing into practice this week:

_____
_____
_____
_____
_____
_____
_____
_____
_____
_____
_____
_____
_____
_____
_____
_____
_____
_____
_____

TALKING TO GOD

WEEK FOUR

▶ **MEMORY VERSE**
"My heart says of you, 'Seek his face!' Your face, LORD, I will seek."

(PSALM 27.8 NIV)

WEEK **FOUR** · DAY **ONE**

SEEKING HIS FACE

You were created to know God in a deep and personal way. That kind of relationship requires not only listening to God, but also talking to God through prayer. Maybe in the past you struggled with your prayer life. Maybe you are tired of rote, wooden, repetitive prayers that never really seem to go anywhere or accomplish much. This week you are going to learn how to seek God's face in a way that is life changing.

Every child is born with an innate desire for face time with his parents. In 1978 researchers discovered that children who had a parent who held them, talked to them and got in their face developed properly. But if a child didn't have a parent, or if the face of the person holding the child was expressionless, the child didn't develop properly. The child would become agitated, frustrated and eventually withdraw. Just as you were wired to need face time with other people, you were also created and wired to crave face time with God.

All through the Bible, God calls His people to seek His face. In **(Psalm 80.3, 7, 19 NIV)** we read, *"Restore us, O God; make your face shine on us, that we may be saved. ... Restore us, God Almighty; make your face shine on us, that we may be saved. ... Restore us, LORD God Almighty; make your face shine on us, that we may be saved."*

(2 Chronicles 7.14 NIV) says, *"If my people, who are called by my name, will humble themselves and pray and seek my face and turn from their wicked ways, then I will hear from heaven, and I will forgive their sin and will heal their land."*

(1 Chronicles 16.11 NIV) advises, *"Look to the LORD and his strength; seek his face always."*

(Psalm 89.15 ESV) cries out, *"Blessed are the people who know the festal shout, who walk, O LORD, in the light of your face."*

(Psalm 105.4 NIV) tells us, *"Look to the LORD and his strength; seek his face always."*

The priestly blessing that was spoken over Israel every day at the morning and evening sacrifices stated, *"The LORD bless you and keep you; the LORD make his face to shine upon you and be gracious to you; the LORD lift up his countenance upon you and give you peace,"* **(Numbers 6.24-26 ESV)**. The people would hear it and reply, *"Amen."* Let it be! May God's face shine on us!

That's the invitation. Seek His face.

This week you are invited to seek God's face in prayer, but the invitation requires a response. **(Psalm 27.8 NIV)** says, *"My heart says of you, 'Seek his face!' Your face, LORD, I will seek."*

Will you seek God's face?

THINK IT OUT

What does it mean to seek God's face?

_____
_____
_____
_____
_____
_____
_____
_____
_____

What hinders you from seeking God on a daily basis?

_____
_____
_____
_____
_____
_____
_____
_____
_____
_____
_____
_____

LIVE IT OUT

Begin memorizing your Scripture memory verse for the week:

"My heart says of you, 'Seek his face!' Your face, LORD, I will seek."
(PSALM 27.8 NIV)

Review your *"I Will"* statement for this week.

This week you will begin reading through the **Gospel of Luke**. If you have time each day, I encourage you to read the entire chapter, but if your time is limited, make sure you at least read the focal passage listed below. A medical doctor, Luke, interviewed eyewitnesses and wrote a chronological account of the life of Jesus. Later, Luke helped the Apostle Paul take the message of Jesus around the world, and he also wrote the book of Acts. **The Gospel of Luke** was written in approximately 60 A.D.

Read **(Luke 1.26-38)**.
As you read, remember to **l.i.s.t.e.n.** to God. Underline what stands out to you. Study what you underlined. Meditate on how this applies to your life. Pray what God has spoken to you back to Him as your personal prayer.

Note: pages are available for you to journal what God is saying to you.

PRAY IT OUT

Ask God to give you a fresh desire to seek His face today in prayer.

SAMPLE JOURNAL ENTRY

October 3, 2017 — God made a way for me

Look at Scripture: John 3

Identify what stands out

For God so loved the world that he gave his only Son, that whoever believes in him should not perish but have eternal life John 3:16

Study the Passage:
- God gave his Son for us
- We are to believe in Jesus
- Only through Jesus can we have eternal life

Think deeply how this applies to your life:
- God loves me and made a way for me to be right with Him
- God wants me to believe in, trust in, rely upon Jesus and follow him with all my heart.
- I have eternal life through Jesus alone

Engage in prayer:
Father I praise you because you have made a way for me to know you deeply and personally. Forgive me for the times I don't obey you completely. Please help me to boldly share the good news of your grace with the people around me. Now fill me with your Spirit. Lead me, direct me, and use me. I surrender the control of my life to you.

Note what God says in your journal
Summarize the key thought by adding a title at the top of the page.

DAY ONE JOURNAL ENTRY

Look. Identify. Study. Think deeply. Engage in prayer. Note what God says.

WEEK **FOUR** · DAY **TWO**

WHY PRAY?

Some people struggle when it comes to prayer. I remember talking with a man who said, *"I can pray for my friends and family, but I don't feel worthy to ask God to do anything for me."* Another person told me, *"I stopped praying because I didn't see it doing any good."* One man said, *"God is going to do what He's going to do, so there is no use praying."* Most of these comments stem from a misunderstanding about prayer.

What is prayer? Prayer is simply talking with God.

In **(Exodus 33.11 NIV)**, we read that Moses talked to God personally, *"The LORD would speak to Moses face to face, as one speaks to a friend."* The phrase "face to face" indicates normal conversation, just like you would talk to a friend. That is what God wants from you. He wants you to seek Him and talk to Him, not in rote and memorized words, but from your heart.

Throughout the Bible God calls us to seek Him and talk to Him. Prayer is more about relationship than results. When we pray, He promises to hear us, respond to our needs and draw us close to Him. Consider these benefits of prayer:

God promises to give you peace. *"Do not be anxious about anything, but in every situation, by prayer and petition, with thanksgiving, present your requests to God. And the peace of God, which transcends all understanding, will guard your hearts and your minds in Christ Jesus,"* **(Philippians 4.6-7 NIV)**.

God promises to hear you and to help you. *"Let us then approach God's throne of grace with confidence, so that we may receive mercy and find grace to help us in our time of need,"* **(Hebrews 4.16 NIV)**.

God promises to respond in the way that is best for you. *"Which of you, if your son asks for bread, will give him a stone? Or if he asks for a fish, will give him a snake? If you, then, though you are evil, know how to give good gifts to your children, how much more will your Father in heaven give good gifts to those who ask him!,"* **(Matthew 7.9-11 NIV)**.

God promises to give you a new perspective. In **(Psalm 73)**, the psalmist was struggling with injustice in the world. Consequently, he had become a "brute beast" — angry, resentful, insensitive to God. Then he came into God's presence in prayer and God changed his perspective. *"My flesh and my heart may fail, but God is the strength of my heart and my portion forever,"* **(Psalm 73.26 NIV)**.

God promises rest. In **(Matthew 11.28 NIV)** Jesus said, *"Come to me, all you who are weary and burdened, and I will give you rest."*

God promises to be close to you. *"The LORD is near to the brokenhearted and saves those who are crushed in spirit,"* **(Psalm 34.18 NASB)**.

God promises power to overcome. The Apostle Paul was discouraged and lonely. Jesus said, *"My grace is sufficient for you, for power is perfected in weakness,"* **(2 Corinthians 12.9 NASB)**.

THINK IT OUT

What questions do you have about prayer?

_____
_____
_____
_____
_____
_____
_____
_____
_____

Which one of these promises means the most to you right now?

_____
_____
_____
_____
_____
_____
_____
_____
_____

LIVE IT OUT

Review your Scripture memory verse for the week:

"My heart says of you, 'Seek his face!' Your face, LORD, I will seek."
(PSALM 27.8 NIV)

Review your *"I Will"* statement for this week.

Read **(Luke 2.1-21)**.
Continue to **l.i.s.t.e.n.** to God as you read.

PRAY IT OUT

Spend time thanking God for His many promises.

DAY TWO JOURNAL ENTRY

Look. **I**dentify. **S**tudy. **T**hink deeply. **E**ngage in prayer. **N**ote what God says.

WEEK **FOUR** · DAY **THREE**

PRAISE GOD

Jesus was a man of prayer. He was consumed with prayer and intimacy with the Father. On thirty-three different occasions in the Gospels, Jesus pulled away from the crowd to pray. Take a look at this brief snapshot of Jesus' prayer life:

- Jesus began His ministry in extended prayer.
- The Spirit fell on Jesus at His baptism as He prayed.
- Jesus changed the course of His ministry after times of prayer.
- After prayer, Jesus walked on water and challenged Peter to get out of the boat.
- After a time of prayer, Jesus showed compassion to a woman caught in adultery.
- During a time of prayer, Jesus was transfigured before His disciples.
- After a night of prayer, Jesus chose His leadership team.
- After a time of prayer, Jesus was strengthened to endure the cross.
- Because of prayer and fasting, Jesus was able to overcome demons.
- Jesus often retreated with His team for times of prayer.
- Jesus' last words on the cross were prayers.
- Jesus' last instructions for the disciples were to return to Jerusalem and to pray.

Jesus' whole life was consumed with prayer, and the disciples noticed it was His prayer life that brought power. At one point they approached Jesus and asked Him to teach them to pray. We never see the disciples asking Jesus to teach them to preach or do miracles, but we see them hungry to learn how to pray like Jesus. *"Pray then like this,"* Jesus said. *"Our Father in heaven, hallowed be your name. Your kingdom come, your will be done, on earth as it is in heaven. Give us this day our daily bread, and forgive us our debts, as we also have forgiven our debtors. And lead us not into temptation, but deliver us from evil,"* **(Matthew 6.9-13 ESV)**.

People often call this *"The Lord's Prayer,"* but it should be called, *"The Model Prayer,"* because Jesus is giving us a model of how to pray. You can take this model and break it down into four letters that are easy to remember: **P.R.A.Y.**

P stands for **PRAISE**. Jesus begins His prayer with praising the Father. He said *"Our Father in heaven, hallowed be your name,"* **(Matthew 6.9 ESV)**. Hallowed means holy, set apart or to revere something or someone. Jesus is saying, *"Father, your name is Holy!"* Jesus began His prayer with praise. The first thing you need to do when you come into God's presence is praise.

(Psalm 100.4 NIV) says, *"Enter his gates with thanksgiving and his courts with praise; give thanks to him and praise his name."* **(Psalm 22.3 ESV)** says that *"Yet you are holy, enthroned on the praises of Israel."* The angels are in God's presence crying out, *"Holy, Holy, Holy is the LORD Almighty, the whole earth is full of his glory,"* **(Isaiah 6.3 NIV)**. If that's true, then when you come into God's presence, you don't come with your hands out, you come with your hands up, praising Him!

Why is it important to praise God first when you pray? First, praise puts God center stage. When you praise Him, you acknowledge who He is and what He has done. You come before your God and King with awe and reverence and gratitude.

Second, praise makes you aware of God's presence. When the people praised God, the presence of God filled the temple, **(2 Chronicles 5.13-14 ESV)**. When we praise God, we sense His presence with us. Most of the time, you don't need to rehearse your problems in prayer. What you really need is a fresh vision of God and His presence with you in the midst of your troubles.

Third, praise is our battle stance. Satan hates it when you praise God. When you begin to pray, you are going to face opposition, but the battle begins and ends in praise. King Jehoshaphat marched into battle with the choir out on the front lines because he knew that God was going to show up when His people began to worship Him, **(2 Chronicles 20.21 ESV)**. Praising God is the first step to dynamic prayer.

THINK IT OUT

What stands out most to you about Jesus' prayer life? Why?

___
___
___
___
___
___

Why do you think Jesus put praise as the first step in prayer?

_____
_____
_____
_____
_____
_____
_____
_____
_____

LIVE IT OUT

Review your Scripture memory verse for the week:

"My heart says of you, 'Seek his face!' Your face, LORD, I will seek."
(PSALM 27.8 NIV)

Review your *"I Will"* statement for this week.

Read **(Luke 3.1-9)**. Continue to **l.i.s.t.e.n.** to God as you read.

PRAY IT OUT

Spend time praising God today. Don't ask for anything; just praise Him and thank Him for what He has done for you.

DAY THREE JOURNAL ENTRY

Look. Identify. Study. Think deeply. Engage in prayer. Note what God says.

WEEK **FOUR** · DAY **FOUR**

RETURN

If **P** stands for praise, then **R** stands for **RETURN.** How can I return to God and find forgiveness and mercy?

Prayer begins with praise, but Jesus moved from praise to another important component of prayer. In His model prayer He continued, *"Your kingdom come, your will be done, on earth as it is in heaven,"* **(Matthew 6.10 ESV)**.

Why did Jesus pray for the kingdom to come and the Father's will to be done? The kingdom of God is mentioned 103 times in the Bible and is a very important concept. When you think of a kingdom, your mind immediately goes to geographic boundaries and territories, but God's kingdom isn't about land and boundaries. When questioned by Pilate, the Roman governor, Jesus said: *"My kingdom is not of this world,"* **(John 18.36 ESV)**.

God's kingdom is something different. Here's a definition: The kingdom of God is the rule of God in the lives of His people. To be part of God's kingdom is to do His will, and those who do God's will are part of His kingdom. So when you pray, *"Your kingdom come, your will be done,"* you are praying: *"Father, right now I want you to rule in my life. Just for today, I submit my life to your loving leadership. I surrender my will to your perfect will. I acknowledge and come under your authority because you know what is best for me. I don't want to go my way; I want to go your way, Father. I want to fulfill your purpose for my life."*

Unfortunately, the truth is that we often don't live that way. There are many areas of our lives where we go outside of God's will. We sin. We fail. We struggle. We wander. That's why we need to return to the Lord.

In Psalm 51, King David is returning to God. Though his secret sin entangled him, and his choices sent him drifting far from God, David was making his way home.

Take an honest inventory. David said, *"Surely I was sinful at birth, sinful from the time my mother conceived me,"* **(Psalm 51.5 NIV)**. David understood that there was a natural tendency in him to sin. That sinful tendency is in all of us. In **(Psalm 139.23-24 NLT)** David prayed, *"Search me, O God, and know my heart; test me and know my anxious thoughts. Point out anything in me that offends you, and lead me along the path of everlasting life."* Returning begins with asking God to show you the areas of your life that veer outside the loving boundaries of His will.

Confess your sin to God. Confessing your sin means to see it the way God sees it. Listen to David's words: *"For I know my transgressions, and my sin is always before me. Against you, you only, have I sinned and done what is evil in your sight; so you are right in your verdict and justified when you judge,"* **(Psalm 51.3-4 NIV)**. David's not minimizing, he's not making excuses, he's not blame shifting — he's owning his sin. He is beginning to see that his sin is an affront to a holy God who loves him! **(Proverbs 28.13 NIV)** says, *"Whoever conceals their sins does not prosper, but the one who confesses and renounces them finds mercy."*

Ask God to forgive you. David prays, *"Have mercy on me, O God, according to your unfailing love; according to your great compassion blot out my transgressions,"* **(Psalm 51.1 NIV)**. The whole Bible can be summed up in one word: forgiveness. We all have sinned against God. We all deserve God's judgment. But, God loved you so much that He sent His only Son, Jesus Christ, to die on a cross in your place to pay the penalty for your sin. If you will look to Jesus, confess your sin and return to Him, He will forgive you.

Accept God's cleansing work in your life. Look at David's description of a forgiven person: *"Wash away all my iniquity and cleanse me from my sin,"* **(Psalm 51.2 NIV)**. *"Cleanse me with hyssop, and I will be clean; wash me, and I will be whiter than snow,"* **(Psalm 51.7 NIV)**. *"Create in me a pure heart, O God,"* **(Psalm 51.10 NIV)**. A forgiven person is clean on the inside. **(1 John 1.8-9 NIV)** says, *"If we claim to be without sin, we deceive ourselves and the truth is not in us. If we confess our sins, he is faithful and just and will forgive us our sins and purify us from all unrighteousness."*

THINK IT OUT

Why do you think confessing your sin to God in prayer is important?

_____
_____
_____
_____
_____
_____
_____
_____
_____
_____

What keeps you from returning to the Lord?

___
___
___
___
___
___
___
___
___
___

LIVE IT OUT

Review your Scripture memory verse for the week:

"My heart says of you, 'Seek his face!' Your face, LORD, I will seek."
(PSALM 27.8 NIV)

Review your *"I Will"* statement for this week.

Read **(Luke 4.1-13)**. Continue to **l.i.s.t.e.n.** to God as you read.

PRAY IT OUT

Spend time confessing to God. Ask Him to search you and show you any area that is outside of His desire for your life.

DAY FOUR JOURNAL ENTRY

Look. Identify. Study. Think deeply. Engage in prayer. Note what God says.

WEEK **FOUR** · DAY **FIVE**

ASK

Prayer starts with praise. Prayer involves returning to God in confession. Then prayer moves to our needs. The **A** in our acrostic **P.R.A.Y.** stands for **ASK**.

God wants you to come to Him and ask for the things you need. Jesus said, *"Keep on asking, and you will receive what you ask for. Keep on seeking, and you will find. Keep on knocking, and the door will be opened to you. For everyone who asks, receives. Everyone who seeks, finds. And to everyone who knocks, the door will be opened,"* **(Matthew 7.7-8 NLT)**.

Jesus asked His Father for several things, and in prayer you can ask for these same things as well. In the Lord's model prayer, Jesus used plural pronouns such as *"our"*, *"us"* and *"we"*. In doing so Jesus reminds us that as we ask for our heavenly Father to meet our needs, we can also ask Him to meet the needs of others as we pray for them.

What should you ask God to provide for you?

Ask for provision. *"Give us this day our daily bread,"* **(Matthew 6.11 ESV)**. Asking for daily bread meant relying on God's provision for the day. As you pray in the morning, ask God to provide what you need that day. It may be material (food, shelter, clothing). It may be practical (a new job, to make a sale). It may be emotional (strength to fight for your marriage, wisdom in raising your kids, patience with your boss). It may be spiritual (peace, joy, boldness). Pray with your schedule in mind. Pray for the things you will face that day and ask God to be your Provider.

Ask for personal relationships. *"And forgive us our debts, as we also have forgiven our debtors,"* **(Matthew 6.12 ESV)**. Why does Jesus add this here? Because your relationships with people affect your relationship with God. You can't expect God to forgive you while you are holding a grudge against another person. Jesus said, *"If you forgive those who sin against you, your heavenly Father will forgive you,"* **(Matthew 6.14 NLT)**. He even went so far as to say, *"You have heard that it was said, 'Love your neighbor and hate your enemy.' But I tell you, love your enemies and pray for those who persecute you,"* **(Matthew 5.43-44 NIV)**. Pray for health in your relationships and the strength to forgive those who have hurt you.

Ask for protection. *"And lead us not into temptation, but deliver us from the evil one,"* **(Matthew 6.13 NIV)**. The word temptation here comes from the Greek word *peirasmon* meaning "a trial or a test." The idea here is not, "God don't lead me into a place where I'm tempted to do evil," but rather, "don't lead me into a trial or test where Satan may attack me." **(1 Peter 5.8 NIV)** says, *"Be alert and of sober mind. Your enemy the devil prowls around like a roaring lion looking for someone to devour."* We live in a dangerous world. Our enemy is on the prowl, looking for someone to eat! He's on the prowl in troubles, trials, difficulties — looking for an opportunity to destroy your faith, cause you to question God, wreck your home and marriage and make you feel worthless and isolated. Jesus was saying, "Pray for protection. Pray for God's leadership to help you avoid falling into the devil's traps."

As you ask for these things, remember that your Heavenly Father loves you and wants to provide for you. In **(Luke 11.11-13 ESV)** Jesus said, *"What father among you, if his son asks for a fish, will instead of a fish give him a serpent; or if he asks for an egg, will give him a scorpion? If you then, who are evil, know how to give good gifts to your children, how much more will the heavenly Father give the Holy Spirit to those who ask him!"*

Pray daily for your needs. Pray specifically, not in generalities. Pray persistently and don't quit. And pray expecting God to move. **(1 John 5.14 NIV)** says, *"This is the confidence we have in approaching God: that if we ask anything according to his will, he hears us."*

THINK IT OUT

In what ways are you asking God to provide for you?

_____
_____
_____
_____
_____
_____
_____
_____
_____
_____
_____

What hinders you the most from asking God to meet your needs?

_____
_____
_____
_____
_____
_____
_____
_____
_____

LIVE IT OUT

Review your Scripture memory verse for the week:

"My heart says of you, 'Seek his face!' Your face, LORD, I will seek."
(PSALM 27.8 NIV)

Review your *"I Will"* statement for this week.

Read **(Luke 5.1-11)**. Continue to **l.i.s.t.e.n.** to God as you read.

PRAY IT OUT

Spend time asking God to provide for you and meet your needs.

DAY FIVE JOURNAL ENTRY

Look. Identify. Study. Think deeply. Engage in prayer. Note what God says.

WEEK **FOUR** · DAY **SIX**

YIELD

If **P** stands for praise, **R** stands for return and **A** stands for ask, then **Y** stands for **YIELD**. Just as a yield sign indicates you should let someone else go ahead of you, in our walk with God, yield means we surrender our lives to Jesus and commit to follow Him and let Him lead.

If you look at **(Matthew 6.13 ESV)**, right away you will notice that you don't see the normal benediction of the Lord's prayer. However, most Bibles will have a footnote that reads, *"For yours is the kingdom and the power and the glory forever. Amen."*

You may say, *"Why is this part of the Lord's Prayer in a footnote?"* Remember that the New Testament Gospels were the most copied documents in the ancient world. Unlike today, where we would just print more copies or use a copier, at that time every copy was created meticulously by hand. These copies were called manuscripts. While most of the manuscript evidence dating back as early as the end of the first century supports this portion of the Lord's Prayer, there are some earlier manuscripts that omit it. That's why it is not included in our Bible, but in the footnote.

That being said, it is almost unthinkable that a Jew would not close a prayer in praise to God. It was a common practice. For example, King David prayed this: *"Yours, LORD, is the greatness and the power and the glory and the majesty and the splendor, for everything in heaven and earth is yours. Yours, LORD, is the kingdom; you are exalted as head over all,"* **(1 Chronicles 29.11 NIV)**.

When we come to the end of the Lord's Prayer and pray these words, *"[For Yours is the kingdom and the power and the glory forever. Amen.]"* **(Matthew 6.13 NASB)**, you are saying, *"Lord, I yield to you in every part of my life. This is all about you, your kingdom, your power, your glory!"* It's a statement of yielding to God.

Yielding means I acknowledge God's sovereign authority in my life. *"Lord, I may not understand all that is happening around me, but you are King. You are in control. You are the undisputed leader and authority over me. You are sovereign over my life. No matter what happens, I recognize and yield to your authority and sovereignty in my life."*

As long as you are fighting God, you are fighting a losing battle. Pastor and author Ron Dunn experienced several challenges in life. Each time, he saw every hardship as an opportunity to trust God and draw near to Jesus. Often he would quote **(Ecclesiastes 5.2 NIV)**, *"God is in heaven and you are on earth, so let your words be few."* There are some things we will never understand this side of heaven. Some things we don't see from our perspective. But God is in control so we yield to his plan and pray, *"Lord, whatever you want, whenever you want, wherever you want – that's what I want."*

Yielding means I surrender to the Spirit's power in my life. *"Lord, you are all powerful, and I want you to fill me with your Spirit."* God wants to pour His power into your life — power to change, power to endure, power to live for Him — but He is looking for open vessels to fill. Each morning pray, *"Lord fill me, Lord change me, Lord use me, Lord lead me, Lord control me — I'm yours."*

Yielding means living your life for God's glory and not your own. *"Lord, life isn't about me. It isn't about my comfort, my convenience, my glory or what people think about me. True life is reflecting your glory."* **(1 Corinthians 10.31 NIV)** says, *"So whether you eat or drink or whatever you do, do it all for the glory of God."*

THINK IT OUT

What does it mean for you to yield to God?

_____
_____
_____
_____
_____
_____
_____
_____
_____
_____
_____
_____
_____
_____

What most often keeps you from yielding to God?

___

LIVE IT OUT

Review your Scripture memory verse for the week:

"My heart says of you, 'Seek his face!' Your face, LORD, I will seek."
(PSALM 27.8 NIV)

Review your *"I Will"* statement for this week.

Read **(Luke 6.12-36)**. Continue to **l.i.s.t.e.n.** to God as you read.

PRAY IT OUT

Spend time asking God to provide for you and meet your needs.

DAY SIX JOURNAL ENTRY

Look. Identify. Study. Think deeply. Engage in prayer. Note what God says.

WEEK **FOUR** · DAY **SEVEN**

HINDRANCES TO PRAYER

Have you ever prayed and didn't see results? I believe the Bible teaches that God always answers our prayers. Sometime His answer is *"yes"* and we see His visible provision. Sometimes His answer is *"no"* because our prayers are not aligned with His plans. Sometimes His answer is *"not yet"* because the timing is not right to answer that prayer. But in every case, your Heavenly Father answers prayer.

There are, however, some things that can hinder your prayers from being answered. These things restrict your prayers and render them ineffective:

Wrong motives
"And even when you ask, you don't get it because your motives are all wrong — you want only what will give you pleasure," **(James 4.3 NLT)**.

Secret sin
"If I had not confessed the sin in my heart, the Lord would not have listened," **(Psalm 66.18 NLT)**.

Dishonoring relationships
"In the same way, you husbands must give honor to your wives. Treat your wife with understanding as you live together. She may be weaker than you are, but she is your equal partner in God's gift of new life. Treat her as you should so your prayers will not be hindered," **(1 Peter 3.7 NLT)**.

Idols in our hearts
"Son of man, these leaders have set up idols in their hearts. They have embraced things that will make them fall into sin. Why should I listen to their requests?," **(Ezekiel 14.3 NLT)**.

Lack of faith
"He could not do any miracles there, except lay his hands on a few sick people and heal them. He was amazed at their lack of faith," **(Mark 6.5-6 NIV)**.

Lack of forgiveness
"If you forgive those who sin against you, your heavenly Father will forgive you. But if you refuse to forgive others, your Father will not forgive your sins." **(Matthew 6.14-15 NLT)**.

THINK IT OUT

Which of these hindrances to prayer stand out the most to you?

_____
_____
_____
_____
_____

How can you avoid these hindrances to prayer?

_____
_____
_____
_____
_____

LIVE IT OUT

Review your Scripture memory verse for the week:

"My heart says of you, 'Seek his face!' Your face, LORD, I will seek."
(PSALM 27.8 NIV)

Review your *"I Will"* statement for this week.

Take the day to review the notes you made through your reading in Luke. Reflect on what God has spoken to you.

PRAY IT OUT

Spend time asking God to show you anything that would hinder your prayers.

FOR GROUP TIME
My *"I Will"* Statement:
As a result of what I have just studied, I will put this one thing into practice this week:

DAY SEVEN JOURNAL ENTRY

Look. Identify. Study. Think deeply. Engage in prayer. Note what God says.

OBEYING GOD

WEEK FIVE

▶ **MEMORY VERSE**

"Whoever has my commandments and keeps them, he it is who loves me. And he who loves me will be loved by my Father, and I will love him and manifest myself to him."

(JOHN 14.21 ESV)

WEEK **FIVE** · DAY **ONE**

GOD'S LOVE LANGUAGE

In 1992, a book was published that took off like wildfire. To date, it has sold more than 10 million copies, has been translated into 50 different languages, and earned a spot on Amazon's top 100 best seller's list of all time. That book is *"The 5 Love Languages"*, by Dr. Gary Chapman.

A counselor and pastor, Dr. Chapman describes five ways through which people receive love — words of affirmation, touch, gifts, acts of service and quality time. I can remember this book having a powerful impact on my marriage as Liz and I tried to apply these principles to our relationship. What stood out most to us was the fact that every person has a primary love language. Every person has a unique way he or she receives love. The other ways are good — and we enjoy them — but there is one way that stands out above the rest that really touches our hearts.

Did you know that God also has a love language? There is one primary way He receives love from you, one way that touches His heart. On the night before His death, Jesus gathered with His men in an upper room. His heart was heavy because they would never meet like this again. In that darkened room, with shadows dancing on the ceiling, Jesus spoke about His love language. He said ...

"If you love me, you will keep my commandments," **(John 14.15 ESV)**.

"Whoever has my commandments and keeps them, he it is who loves me," **(John 14.21 ESV)**.

"If anyone loves me, he will keep my word," **(John 14.23 ESV)**.

Did you see it? Three times Jesus said, *"If you love me, you will do what I'm commanding you to do."*

I want you to notice what He did not say. He did not say:

"If you love me, you will worship me."

"If you love me, you will serve me."

"If you love me, you will read and know the Bible."

"If you love me you will give financially."

Are those things good? Yes. Does God receive those things as good? Yes. But if you do all of those things but not the primary thing, then it doesn't matter to Him.

What shows Jesus that you truly love Him — what touches His heart more than anything else — is when you do what He has commanded you to do! One proves the other!

Your love for God and obedience to Jesus cannot be separated. I know people who say, *"I love God,"* but their lives are not lined up with what Jesus clearly teaches. They claim to love God, but they are harboring bitterness, they spew out anger, they are driven by greed, they ignore the Great Commission — you name it. There is very little obedience to King Jesus in their lives. There is something wrong with this picture.

Jesus is saying, *"What's wrong with the picture is a heart issue. They don't really love me."* Over 28 times in the Gospels, Jesus commands His followers to listen to Him and do what He says. *"Listen carefully." "Hear my words." "Do what I say." "Obey my commands." "Act on what I say."*

Obedience is a big deal to Jesus, but it's seen as optional today. I believe that the heart of the problem of why so many Christians are not experiencing the abundant, overflowing, God-blessed, joyful life that Jesus wants to give them is because of this one problem. Many really do not love Him enough to obey Him.

In the upper room, Jesus was sharing His last words with the men He had loved and poured His life into for more than three years. Last words are really important. In that moment He said, *"Men, it is really important that you live a life of obedience to me!"*

You may ask *"Why? Why should I alter my life to obey Jesus?"* It's like the conversation when a parent tells a child to do something and the kid asks, *"Why?"* Usually the parent will say something like, *"Because I told you so!"* Well, Jesus could have said that. He could have said, *"Obey me because I'm your King!"* But He didn't. In this passage He actually says, *"If you really love me and you alter your life to obey me, I will bless you."*

Through obedience you experience the power of the Spirit **(John 14.15-17 ESV)**, the love of the Father **(John 14.21, 23 ESV)**, and the nearness of Christ in your life **(John 14.21, 23 ESV)**. Do you want to experience all that God has for your life? You can, but these things come pouring into your life through the funnel of obedience. This week we are going to look at what it means to live a life of obedience to Jesus.

THINK IT OUT

Why do you think obedience is God's love language?

___

___

___

___

What is the relationship between love and obedience?

___

LIVE IT OUT

Begin memorizing your Scripture memory verse for the week:

"Whoever has my commandments and keeps them, he it is who loves me. And he who loves me will be loved by my Father, and I will love him and manifest myself to him."
(JOHN 14.21 ESV)

Review your *"I Will"* statement for this week.

Read **(Luke 7:36-50)**. Continue to **l.i.s.t.e.n.** to God as you read and **p.r.a.y.**

PRAY IT OUT

Ask God to help you obey Him in every area of your life.

DAY ONE JOURNAL ENTRY

Look. **I**dentify. **S**tudy. **T**hink deeply. **E**ngage in prayer. **N**ote what God says.

Praise. **R**eturn. **A**sk. **Y**ield.

WEEK **FIVE** · DAY **TWO**

THE OBEDIENCE OF JESUS

Obedience is God's love language, and Jesus was the perfect example of how to love God and obey Him completely. Jesus made it very clear that His focus was on obeying His Father only. He said, *"The one who sent me is with me; he has not left me alone, for I always do what pleases him,"* **(John 8.29 NIV)**.

That word *"always"* is amazing to me. Jesus always did what pleased His Father. He never once skirted the boundary or stepped across the line. He never sinned. This attitude of obedience was forged even as a young man. Jesus chose to be obedient. **(Hebrews 5.7-9 NLT)** gives us a glimpse into Jesus' life, *"While Jesus was here on earth, he offered prayers and pleadings, with a loud cry and tears, to the one who could rescue him from death. And God heard his prayers because of his deep reverence for God. Even though Jesus was God's Son, he learned obedience from the things he suffered. In this way, God qualified him as a perfect High Priest, and he became the source of eternal salvation for all those who obey him."*

Look at the passage again. While Jesus certainly prayed "with a *loud cry and tears*" in the Garden of Gethsemane, I'm convinced that wasn't the first time Jesus had suffered. I'm sure, even as a young boy, Jesus suffered as He chose to obey His Father instead of following the crowd. I'm sure He was tormented and ridiculed even by His own brothers. I mean, how would you like it if perfect Jesus was your older brother?

But every step, every day, Jesus chose to obey God and not men. He chose to bend His life to the Father's will, not the wind of the culture. He learned obedience through suffering. He learned in hard times to stand firm and trust the Father. We know as a young man — most likely twelve to thirteen years old — Jesus was confirmed at His Bar Mitzvah in Jerusalem. Even then, He was aware that He had to be about His Father's business. He had to be obedient to the kingdom agenda of His heavenly Father **(Luke 2.49 ESV)**. In **(Luke 2.40 NLT)** we read, *"There the child grew up healthy and strong. He was filled with wisdom, and God's favor was on him."*

Jesus grew in obedience to His parents and obedience to His heavenly Father. *"Jesus grew in wisdom and in stature and in favor with God and all the people,"* **(Luke 2.52 NLT)**.

Later, Jesus suffered and chose obedience when He was tempted. *"Since he himself has gone through suffering and testing, he is able to help us when we are being tested,"* **(Hebrews 2.18 NLT)**. At the beginning of His ministry, Jesus was tested and tempted by Satan directly **(Luke 4.1-13 ESV)**, and He continued to be tempted and tested throughout His ministry. All the while, Jesus chose to say no to the passing pleasures of sin and say yes to His Father. Jesus said, *"I carry out the will of the one who sent me, not my own will,"* **(John 5.30 NLT)** and also *"I love the Father and do exactly what my Father has commanded me,"* **(John 14.31 NIV)**.

But the obedience of Jesus was most clearly seen on the cross. As He struggled in the garden, He once again — as He had done His whole life — said yes to His Father. *"Father, if you are willing, please take this cup of suffering away from me. Yet I want your will to be done, not mine,"* **(Luke 22.42 NLT)**.

After learning to trust and obey His Father in small trials, Jesus was able to trust and obey His Father in His biggest trial. That is why we are urged to follow the example of Jesus. In **(Philippians 2.5-8 NLT)** the Apostle Paul writes: *"You must have the same attitude that Christ Jesus had. Though he was God, he did not think of equality with God as something to cling to. Instead, he gave up his divine privileges; he took the humble position of a slave and was born as a human being. When he appeared in human form, he humbled himself in obedience to God and died a criminal's death on a cross."*

Jesus is our example of obedience, and He calls us to obey Him completely. On the mountaintop, after His resurrection, Jesus gave His disciples a commission… *"Therefore, go and make disciples of all the nations, baptizing them in the name of the Father and the Son and the Holy Spirit. Teach these new disciples to obey all the commands I have given you. And be sure of this: I am with you always, even to the end of the age,"* **(Matthew 28.19-20 NLT)**. Notice the emphasis. The call of Jesus is to be His disciple, to follow Him and to obey Him with all our hearts — just like He showed us.

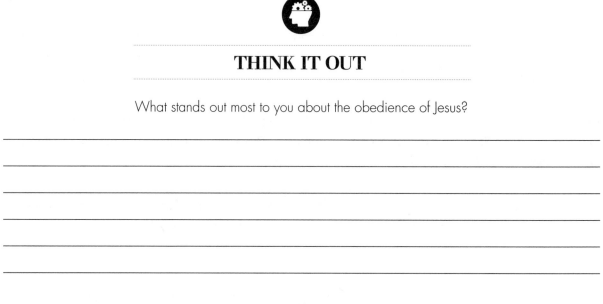

THINK IT OUT

What stands out most to you about the obedience of Jesus?

_____

_____

_____

_____

_____

What would have to change in your life for you to become completely obedient to Jesus?

_____
_____
_____
_____
_____
_____
_____
_____
_____
_____
_____

LIVE IT OUT

Review your Scripture memory verse for the week:

"Whoever has my commandments and keeps them, he it is who loves me. And he who loves me will be loved by my Father, and I will love him and manifest myself to him."
(JOHN 14.21 ESV)

Review your *"I Will"* statement for this week.

Read **(Luke 8:1-15)**. Continue to **l.i.s.t.e.n.** to God as you read and **p.r.a.y.**

PRAY IT OUT

Ask God to remove any barrier that keeps you from obeying Him completely.

DAY TWO JOURNAL ENTRY

Look. Identify. Study. Think deeply. Engage in prayer. Note what God says.

Praise. Return. Ask. Yield.

WEEK **FIVE** · DAY **THREE**

THE REST OF THE GOSPEL

The king was at a crossroads. He had been given a direct command to wipe out the Amalekites. Nothing was to be left standing. But his men were clamoring to keep some of the choice cattle and livestock. Which would he choose?

King Saul was one of the most promising men in Israel. At the time he was anointed the nation's first king, Saul was head and shoulders above the rest — literally. He was tall, strong, intelligent, handsome and God-fearing. He came from a prominent family and a noble tribe. From all outward appearances, Saul was the obvious choice for king.

Early on God was with Saul, defeating the enemies of Israel. Saul was a surging leader with tremendous promise, but the choice he was about to make would determine his destiny. As the prophet Samuel approached King Saul, he knew what choice had been made. The sound of bleating sheep and animals was evidence of Saul's choice.

In **(1 Samuel 15.19 NIV)**, Samuel asked, *"Why did you not obey the LORD? Why did you pounce on the plunder and do evil in the eyes of the LORD?"* Saul admitted that he was afraid and had given in to the demands of his men, but the cattle were only spared to be offered as a sacrifice to the Lord. Then Samuel made this powerful statement... *"Listen! Obedience is better than sacrifice, and submission is better than offering the fat of rams,"* **(1 Samuel 15.22 NLT)**.

Obedience is better. Obedience is better than being religious. Obedience is better than being a good person. Obedience is better than trying your best. Obedience is better, and obedience is what God is looking for in you.

King Saul is a good example of how some people live the Christian life. They feel that once they acknowledge Jesus as the Son of God and turn to Him for salvation, that's the end of the story. They have their sins forgiven and they are going to heaven, so now they can just live their lives as they please. Occasionally they will offer God something — maybe going to worship, reading their Bible, offering to volunteer — but all the while the sound of disobedience is ringing out from their lives.

This is why so many Christians live defeated lives. They want salvation, but not change. They want to know God, but they don't want to obey God. They want God's love, but they don't want Him to be Lord. Is that you? Are there areas of disobedience in your life right now that you are tolerating, even excusing?

Part of the problem is we may not understand the whole gospel. **(Ephesians 2.1-10 ESV)** is a beautiful picture of the gospel. In the first two verses we read that we are dead in our sin, far from God, carrying out our own wayward and sinful desires and headed for divine judgment. But God, being rich in mercy, intervened and though we were dead in sin, He made us alive in Christ, putting His incredible grace on display in our lives. Then we read these words, *"God saved you by his grace when you believed. And you can't take credit for this; it is a gift from God. Salvation is not a reward for the good things we have done, so none of us can boast about it,"* **(Ephesians 2.8-9 NLT)**.

Salvation comes to us when we repent of our sin and place our faith in Jesus Christ alone. We are not saved by our good works; we are saved by His good work done once and for all on the cross. That is where we usually stop reading. We feel that the call of Jesus is simply to believe. But the call of Jesus is to follow Him. In repentance and faith we turn to Jesus, and in obedience we live for Jesus.

Keep reading. *"For we are God's masterpiece. He has created us anew in Christ Jesus, so we can do the good things he planned for us long ago,"* **(Ephesians 2.10 NLT)**. You were created anew to follow Jesus and do good things that He marked off for you to do!

Instead of trusting Jesus and then living your own life, God wants you to trust Jesus and follow Him completely. In **(2 Corinthians 5.15 NLT)** Paul said that *"He died for everyone so that those who receive his new life will no longer live for themselves. Instead, they will live for Christ, who died and was raised for them."*

The normal Christian life is living sold-out for Jesus Christ and obeying Him completely. King Saul forfeited his right to be king that day when he chose to cover his sin instead of obey God. He would never know what kind of king he could have been if he had just obeyed. The same could be said about you. You will never know what great things God could do through your life if you squander it on disobedience. But if you choose to obey Jesus and follow Him, He has great things already planned out for you to do.

THINK IT OUT

How can you compare/contrast King Saul with Jesus?

_____

_____

_____

_____

_____

What does *"following Jesus"* mean to you?

___

LIVE IT OUT

Review your Scripture memory verse for the week:

"Whoever has my commandments and keeps them, he it is who loves me. And he who loves me will be loved by my Father, and I will love him and manifest myself to him."
(JOHN 14.21 ESV)

Review your *"I Will"* statement for this week.

Read **(Luke 9:18-27)**. Continue to **l.i.s.t.e.n.** to God as you read and **p.r.a.y.**

PRAY IT OUT

Praise God that He saved you and has good works prepared for you to do.

DAY THREE JOURNAL ENTRY

Look. **I**dentify. **S**tudy. **T**hink deeply. **E**ngage in prayer. **N**ote what God says.

Praise. **R**eturn. **A**sk. **Y**ield.

WEEK **FIVE** · DAY **FOUR**

LIVING A HOLY LIFE

Obeying Jesus means living a holy life. The term holiness has fallen on hard times these days. Just try avoiding something that might be morally questionable and wait for it. People will say you have a *"holier than thou"* attitude or will call you a *"holy roller."*

The word *"holy"* itself is often misunderstood. What does it mean to be holy? First, you need to understand that God is holy. Holiness is His primary attribute. While the Bible says that God is love or God is merciful, only one attribute of God is repeated three times. In **(Isaiah 6.3 ESV)** the angels shouted in antiphonal praise, *"Holy, holy, holy is the LORD of hosts; the whole earth is full of his glory!"* God declares Himself to be holy in **(Ezekiel 39.7 NIV)**, *"I will no longer let my holy name be profaned, and the nations will know that I the LORD am the Holy One in Israel."*

Holiness means to be completely separate and sinless. The Scriptures tell us that God is sinless and cannot tolerate sin. He is perfectly pure, **(Habakkuk 1.13 ESV)**. He is not like any petty or tribal god, rather He is altogether great and matchless, **(Psalm 40.5 ESV)**.

Holiness pervades all of His attributes. His love is a holy love. His mercy is a holy mercy. His justice is a holy justice. His wrath is a holy wrath. Holiness is what sets Him apart. It is the essence of His complete *"otherness."*

While it's hard to wrap our minds around, holiness is the character and nature of God. Therefore, when God called the Israelites out of the bondage and decay of the pagan Egyptian culture, He called them to be holy like Him. *"For I, the LORD, am the one who brought you up from the land of Egypt, that I might be your God. Therefore, you must be holy because I am holy,"* **(Leviticus 11.45 NLT)**.

They were to be set apart, separate, different, special and distinct from all the other nations of the world. They were set apart to worship and serve God and Him alone. He called them to be different than the pagan culture around them and to obey and serve Him only.

Over time, the Israelites disobeyed God and slipped back into the dark culture around them. But in Christ, God called a new community — His church — to live holy lives. The Apostle Peter writes, *"Don't slip back into your old ways of living to satisfy your own desires. You didn't know any better then. But now you must be holy in everything you do, just as God who chose you is holy. For the Scriptures say, 'You must be holy because I am holy',"* **(1 Peter 1.14-16 NLT)**.

When you came to Christ, He called you to follow Him. Following Him means living a holy life. Actually, the moment you were saved, the sacrifice of Jesus made you perfect. He washed you and cleaned you. From God's perspective, you are already holy. But now as you live your daily life, you strive to live out in practical ways who you already are in God's eyes. **(Hebrews 10.14 NLT)** says, *"For by that one offering he forever made perfect those who are being made holy."*

Did you get that? By the offering of Jesus, you were made perfect, but now by the Spirit's work in your life, you are continually being made holy. That happens one step at a time as you daily obey Jesus and follow Him. In the words of bestselling author Jerry Bridges, *"Obedience is the pathway to holiness."* The more you choose to obey Christ and say no to the allurements of this world, the more you grow in holiness. The more you disobey Christ, the more you fail to live a holy life.

You might ask, *"Why should I pursue holiness?"* First, you should pursue holy living out of gratitude for all Jesus has done for you. When you are truly overwhelmed with the price Jesus paid to redeem you and pull you out of your sin, why would you ever want to go back?

Second, pursuing holiness is motivated by your love for God. Jesus said, *"If you keep my commandments, you will abide in my love,"* **(John 15.10 ESV)**. Loving Jesus leads you to holy living.

Another reason to pursue holiness is usefulness. Only when you are obeying and following Jesus can God use you to your fullest potential. The Apostle Paul told Timothy, his young trainee, that just as there are nice dishes in the cupboard that are set apart for the finest occasions, God wants you to be holy and set apart to be used in a special way. He concludes with this charge; *"If you keep yourself pure, you will be a special utensil for honorable use. Your life will be clean, and you will be ready for the Master to use you for every good work. Run from anything that stimulates youthful lusts. Instead, pursue righteous living, faithfulness, love, and peace. Enjoy the companionship of those who call on the Lord with pure hearts,"* **(2 Timothy 2.21-22 NLT)**.

Obedient living leads to holy living, and it all comes down to a choice. It requires choosing to run away from things that are not pleasing to God and choosing to run full stride toward those things that are on God's heart. When you do, God will transform you from the inside out and use you to reflect His love to the world around you.

THINK IT OUT

How would you define holiness?

_____

_____

_____

_____

How would you assess your own pursuit of holiness?

_____
_____
_____
_____

What do you need to run from? What do you need to run to?

_____
_____
_____
_____

LIVE IT OUT

Review your Scripture memory verse for the week:

"Whoever has my commandments and keeps them, he it is who loves me. And he who loves me will be loved by my Father, and I will love him and manifest myself to him."
(JOHN 14.21 ESV)

Review your *"I Will"* statement for this week.

Read **(Luke 10:25-37)**. Continue to **l.i.s.t.e.n.** to God as you read and **p.r.a.y.**

PRAY IT OUT

Take time to confess areas of your life that are not pleasing to Him.

DAY FOUR JOURNAL ENTRY

Look. **I**dentify. **S**tudy. **T**hink deeply. **E**ngage in prayer. **N**ote what God says.

_____
_____
_____
_____
_____
_____
_____
_____
_____
_____
_____
_____
_____
_____
_____
_____
_____
_____
_____
_____
_____
_____
_____
_____
_____

Praise. **R**eturn. **A**sk. **Y**ield.

WEEK **FIVE** · DAY **FIVE**

AGAINST THE FLOW

Aligning with Jesus means standing against the world. In **(1 Peter 1.16-17 NLT)**, Peter quotes from the Old Testament … *"For the Scriptures say, 'You must be holy, because I am holy.'* Then he adds, *"So you must live in reverent fear of him during your time as 'foreigners in the land'."*

He is not speaking about the fear of men, but the fear of God. Notice how believers are described — *"foreigners in the land."* Once you set your life to follow Jesus, you are moving against the grain of the culture around you.

The Bible uses the term *"world"* in three different ways. Sometimes the *"world"* is in reference to the physical planet, **(Hebrews 1.2 ESV)**. Other times the *"world"* refers to the people who live on Earth. For example, in **(John 3.16 ESV)**, *"For God so loved the world,"* the word *"world"* refers to people, not the planet. Other times, *"world"* refers to the wayward and wicked culture that is against God. This *"world"* is what you are up against. This is the culture that hates Jesus, hates the gospel, loves sin and despises anyone who lives for truth.

On the night before His death, Jesus warned His followers that love for God ensures hatred from the world; *"If the world hates you, keep in mind that it hated me first. If you belonged to the world, it would love you as its own. As it is, you do not belong to the world, but I have chosen you out of the world. That is why the world hates you. Remember what I told you; 'A servant is not greater than his master.' If they persecuted me, they will persecute you also. If they obeyed my teaching, they will obey yours also. They will treat you this way because of my name, for they do not know the one who sent me. If I had not come and spoken to them, they would not be guilty of sin; but now they have no excuse for their sin. Whoever hates me hates my Father as well,"* **(John 15.18-23 NIV)**.

If you have ever visited a water park, you are familiar with the *"lazy river."* It's a slow-moving stream that encircles the park. People usually lie on their raft and let the gentle current move them downstream. In fact, the current is so light you may not think there is much current at all. But if you get off your inflatable and actually stand in the *"lazy river"*, you will soon realize that the current is really strong and you have to fight to move against it. Our culture is a current. It is a current of values, thoughts, ideas and standards pushed out into the *"mainstream"* through media, education, business and rhetoric. Many of the values are directly opposed to God's values, and the one who chooses to follow Jesus is the person getting off the inflatable and walking steadily upstream against the current.

Jesus told His men, *"Don't be surprised if this world hates you; it hated me."* He was saying, *"Don't be caught off guard if it's hard to fight the flow; it was hard for me too."* That's why Peter called us *"foreigners in the land."*

Our citizenship is not in this world. The Apostle Paul said, *"But our citizenship is in heaven. And we eagerly await a Savior from there, the Lord Jesus Christ,"* **(Philippians 3.20 NIV)**, and we look forward to *"a building from God, an eternal house in heaven, not built by human hands,"* **(2 Corinthians 5.1 NIV)**.

(Hebrews 11.10 NLT) says, *"Abraham was confidently looking forward to a city with eternal foundations, a city designed and built by God."* You should not expect to enjoy the applause of men if you are living for the applause of heaven, but the difference Jesus has made in you is what makes you attractive to those who are looking for hope. Your love for Jesus and your obedience to Him are light in a dark world as you hold out the gospel.

Paul said, *"Live clean, innocent lives as children of God, shining like bright lights in a world full of crooked and perverse people,"* **(Philippians 2.15 NLT)**.

Jesus said, *"In the same way, let your light shine before others, that they may see your good deeds and glorify your Father in heaven,"* **(Matthew 5.16 NIV)**.

No, you are not of this world, but you are in this world to courageously offer hope. As you obey and follow Jesus, you are letting your light shine.

THINK IT OUT

Do you agree that this world is a current moving against God? Why?

_____
_____
_____
_____
_____
_____
_____

How have you had to resist the culture around you?

___

How do you respond when people react negatively to you because you follow Jesus?

___

LIVE IT OUT

Review your Scripture memory verse for the week:

"Whoever has my commandments and keeps them, he it is who loves me. And he who loves me will be loved by my Father, and I will love him and manifest myself to him."
(JOHN 14.21 ESV)

Review your *"I Will"* statement for this week.

Read **(Luke 11:1-13)**. Continue to **l.i.s.t.e.n.** to God as you read and **p.r.a.y.**

PRAY IT OUT

Ask God to give you boldness to live for Him.

DAY FIVE JOURNAL ENTRY

Look. **I**dentify. **S**tudy. **T**hink deeply. **E**ngage in prayer. **N**ote what God says.

Praise. **R**eturn. **A**sk. **Y**ield.

WEEK **FIVE** · DAY **SIX**

THE LURE OF TEMPTATION

Not only will this world resist you, but this world will also tempt you. The culture will oppose you, and if that doesn't work, it will try to lure you away from following Jesus by enticing you to sin. Jesus experienced both.

Those who opposed Jesus resisted Him outright, but He also was tempted. In both Matthew 4 and Luke 4 we see Jesus facing temptation from Satan himself. We will take a deeper look at these passages tomorrow, but know this… If Jesus faced temptation, you will too.

Where do these temptations come from? We know that temptation to do evil does not come from God. God never tempts us to do what is wrong, **(James 1.13; Luke 11.4 ESV)**.

Look at how James answered that question: *"Temptation comes from our own desires, which entice us and drag us away. These desires give birth to sinful actions. And when sin is allowed to grow, it gives birth to death,"* **(James 1.14-15 NLT)**.

Satan tempts by stirring up our own wayward and wicked desires to do wrong. Notice the aggressive language. When you give in to temptation, you are *"dragged away."* You are no longer in control, but you are under sin's control and that one temptation can lead to devastating results. Thoughts lead to actions. Actions become habits. And habits destroy lives.

You probably know people who thought they could play with temptation only later to be consumed and destroyed by it. There are three main areas where temptation strikes. *"Do not love this world nor the things it offers you, for when you love the world, you do not have the love of the Father in you. For the world offers only a craving for physical pleasure, a craving for everything we see, and pride in our achievements and possessions. These are not from the Father, but are from this world,"* **(1 John 2.15-16 NLT)**.

The areas in which we are most vulnerable to temptation are physical pleasure, the constant craving for more things, and pride for what we have and what we've done. John is saying, *"these longings don't come from God, but are shaped by the culture around us."* Behind it all is an intentional plan to destroy you and draw you away from Jesus.

Peter warns, *"Stay alert! Watch out for your great enemy, the devil. He prowls around like a roaring lion, looking for someone to devour,"* **(1 Peter 5.8 NLT)**. The struggle is real. The enemy is resolute and determined, but you can stand under temptation because God has provided you a way out.

Notice what Paul says about every temptation you face: *"The temptations in your life are no different from what others experience. And God is faithful. He will not allow the temptation to be more than you can stand. When you are tempted, he will show you a way out so that you can endure,"* **(1 Corinthians 10.13 NLT)**.

The temptations you face are common to everyone. Your enemy is not very creative. He uses the same temptations over and over. We all face them, but notice – God is faithful. Faithful means 100 percent. That means that God is faithful 100 percent of the time!

Faithful to do what? God is faithful to ensure that you are never tempted beyond what you can handle in His power. He is faithful to show you a way out every time you are tempted. There will always be an exit sign; you just have to take it.

THINK IT OUT

Where does temptation come from?

_____
_____
_____
_____
_____
_____

Do you agree with the three areas where we are most vulnerable to temptation? Why?

_____
_____
_____
_____
_____
_____
_____

Have you seen a way out when you have been tempted in the past? Explain.

___

LIVE IT OUT

Review your Scripture memory verse for the week:

"Whoever has my commandments and keeps them, he it is who loves me. And he who loves me will be loved by my Father, and I will love him and manifest myself to him."
(JOHN 14.21 ESV)

Review your *"I Will"* statement for this week.

Read **(Luke 12:22-34)**. Continue to **l.i.s.t.e.n.** to God as you read and **p.r.a.y.**

PRAY IT OUT

Take time to yield the control of your life over to God today, asking Him to provide His power to overcome temptation.

DAY SIX JOURNAL ENTRY

Look. Identify. Study. Think deeply. Engage in prayer. Note what God says.

Praise. Return. Ask. Yield.

WEEK **FIVE** · DAY **SEVEN**

OVERCOMING TEMPTATION

Everyone is tempted, but how you handle temptation is very important to your walk with Jesus, and your own spiritual health. Maybe you have been fighting the same temptation for years without being able to shake it off. It's like a broken record of temptation – sin, regret, repeat.

How do you break that cycle? I encourage you today to stop and read the temptation of Jesus found in Luke 4. Jesus gives us a great model for overcoming temptation.

Notice when temptation comes. Jesus was tired, hungry, alone and coming off a spiritual high of just being baptized. He was at the beginning of launching His ministry. He was in the wilderness, which was known in the Jewish culture to be a place where demonic spirits dwelt. In the same way, many times we face temptations when we are physically stressed (hungry or tired), when we are alone, when we are doing a good work for God, or when we are in places where temptation to sin can most easily occur.

Think about the times you are most often tempted. When does it happen? What are the circumstances? When temptation comes, your response is to resist. **(James 4.7 NIV)** says, *"Submit yourselves, then, to God. Resist the devil, and he will flee from you."*

Here are some ways to resist the devil when you are tempted:

Avoid environments where you are easily tempted.
"Don't do as the wicked do, and don't follow the path of evildoers. Don't even think about it; don't go that way. Turn away and keep moving," **(Proverbs 4.14-15 NLT)**. If you are going to the places where temptation will most likely occur, then you are headed down the wrong road. Avoid those places. Avoid those people. They will only lead to trouble.

When facing temptation, get away quickly.
"Run from anything that stimulates youthful lusts. Instead, pursue righteous living, faithfulness, love, and peace. Enjoy the companionship of those who call on the Lord with pure hearts," **(2 Timothy 2.22 NLT)**. The key word there is *"run."* First, circle the words *"Run from."* Run from anything that entices you to sin. Don't stop! Don't think about it! Don't hesitate! Run! Just as Joseph ran from the arms of a wayward wife, you need to run from tempting situations, **(Genesis 39.11-12 ESV)**. Second, you need to *"run toward."* Circle the words *"pursue righteous living."* These are the things that you know please God, like faithfulness, love and peace in your life. Finally, you need to *"run with."* Circle the phrase *"Enjoy the companionship of those who call on the Lord."* You need to run with the right people. Remember that who you befriend is who you become.

Replace tempting thoughts with God's Word.
Usually when you are tempted, a thought first comes to mind. The more you think about the temptation (even thinking about how you need to avoid it), the more power it has. Knowing that your thoughts are the first seed of every temptation **(James 1.14-15; 2 Corinthians 10.5 ESV)**, you must replace those thoughts with God's Word. Instead of thinking about the temptation, set your mind on God's Word. Find Scriptures that speak directly about the temptation you are facing. Find Scriptures that remind you of God's faithfulness and His promises. Post these Scriptures around you. Read them aloud. Memorize them. **(Psalm 119.9, 11 NIV)** says, *"How can a young person stay on the path of purity? By living according to your word. … I have hidden your word in my heart that I might not sin against you."*

You hide God's Word in your heart when you memorize and meditate on it day by day, moment by moment. This is what Jesus did. Each time He was tempted by Satan, Jesus responded by quoting Scripture! The Apostle Paul says that Scripture is the *"sword of the Spirit,"* **(Ephesians 6.17 ESV)**. The word *"sword"* isn't a large saber, but a small dagger used for hand-to-hand combat. Take the promises of God and use them strategically against your enemy! Paul again writes, *"Fix your thoughts on what is true, and honorable, and right, and pure, and lovely, and admirable. Think about things that are excellent and worthy of praise. Keep putting into practice all you learned and received from me — everything you heard from me and saw me doing. Then the God of peace will be with you,"* **(Philippians 4.8-9 NLT)**.

Pray for God to help you.
"But the Lord is faithful, and he will strengthen you and protect you from the evil one," **(2 Thessalonians 3.3 NIV)**. This is a wonderful promise. When you're resisting temptation, remember God is 100 percent faithful to you. He will strengthen you and protect you. That is why we are told to come boldly into His presence through prayer to find help in our time of need, **(Hebrews 4.16 ESV)**. That is why Jesus Himself encouraged us to pray for protection during times of temptation, **(Matthew 6.13 ESV)**.

Even when you face temptation, know that Jesus Christ is with you. He is able to guard you, protect you, empower you and uphold you. Jesus understands your temptations. He was tempted just like you, **(Hebrews 4.15 ESV)**.

Even now, Jesus is praying to the Father for you, **(Romans 8.34; Hebrews 7.25 ESV)**. He is more than able to defeat this temptation through His Spirit that is at work in you, **(1 John 4.4 ESV)**. *"Now to him who *is able to keep you from stumbling and to present you blameless before the presence of his glory with great joy, to the only God, our Savior, through Jesus Christ our Lord, be glory, majesty, dominion, and authority, before all time and now and forever. Amen,"* **(Jude 24-25 ESV)**.

THINK IT OUT

How can you avoid places where you are most vulnerable to temptation?

___
___
___
___
___
___
___

What can you do to replace tempting thoughts?

___
___
___
___
___
___
___

Who are you *"running with"*? Are they leading you in the right direction or not?

___
___
___
___
___
___
___

LIVE IT OUT

Review your Scripture memory verse for the week:

"Whoever has my commandments and keeps them, he it is who loves me. And he who loves me will be loved by my Father, and I will love him and manifest myself to him."
(JOHN 14.21 ESV)

Review your *"I Will"* statement for this week.

Take the day to review the notes you made through your reading in Luke.
Reflect on what God has spoken to you.

PRAY IT OUT

Thank God today that He is more than able to help you when temptation comes.

FOR GROUP TIME
*My **"I Will"** Statement:*
As a result of what I have just studied, I will put this one thing into practice this week:

_____
_____
_____
_____
_____
_____
_____

DAY SEVEN JOURNAL ENTRY

Look. Identify. Study. Think deeply. Engage in prayer. Note what God says.

Praise. Return. Ask. Yield.

GOD'S AMAZING
GRACE

WEEK SIX

 **MEMORY VERSE**

"For it is by grace you have been saved, through faith – and this is not from yourselves, it is the gift of God – not by works, so that no one can boast."

(EPHESIANS 2.8-9 NIV)

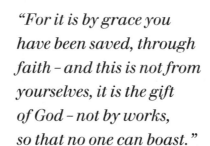

WEEK **SIX** · DAY **ONE**

AMAZING GRACE

John Newton was in trouble. The battering waves and violent winds beat against the bow of his ship to the point that all hope was lost. In utter despair, John cried out, *"Lord, have mercy on us!"*

Reflecting back, those words were the turning point for this wayward man.

John grew up on the ocean. The son of a sailing merchant, John grew up with the breeze in his face and the taste of salt in his mouth. He loved the spray of the ocean and the adventure of sailing to distant lands. By the age of nineteen, John was drafted into service in the British navy. He served on a battleship — the *HMS Harwich* — and was promoted to midshipman. Due to horrible conditions and mistreatment, John deserted his post and was later captured, flogged and demoted.

At his request, John was transferred into service on a slave ship, transporting slaves from the coast of Sierra Leone to England. The slaves were not the only ones to suffer under the brutal treatment of the slave traders; John also was beaten severely and abused. Ultimately, John was able to captain his own ship and continued to benefit financially from the lucrative slave trafficking business.

Up to this point, John had no thought of God and no intention to seek the Lord. That is, until that deadly storm. After the storm passed, John — convinced that God had spared his life — opened his heart once again to the gospel of Jesus Christ. He called that moment his *"great deliverance"* and continued to celebrate May 10, 1748, as his day of salvation. Years later, he was taken under wing by English pastor and evangelist George Whitefield, who taught him how to walk with God and share his faith.

By the age of forty, John had long left his seafaring ways and was in full-time Christian ministry, serving as pastor of several churches in England. People packed the building to hear this once-hardened sinner speak about the grace of God that transformed his life. One of the songs John wrote became one of the greatest hymns of all time. The opening lyrics read, *"Amazing grace! How sweet the sound that saved a wretch like me! I once was lost, but now I'm found; was blind, but now I see."*

John's life was transformed by God's grace. Every life that God touches is an example of His grace. We hear about grace, we sing songs about grace, but what is grace?

The word grace appears 155 times in the New Testament and comes from the Greek word *charis*, which means the undeserved gift of God's favor. Pastor and theologian A.W. Tozer explains, "*Grace is the good pleasure of God that inclines him to bestow benefits on the undeserving,*" (*The Knowledge of the Holy*, New York: Harper & Row, 1961, pg. 100).

At the core, grace is all about God's favor. Many times grace is called a gift from God. The Apostle Paul wrote that we are ***"justified by his grace as a gift, through the redemption that is in Christ Jesus,"*** **(Romans 3.24 ESV)**.

If grace is a gift from God, then that tells us something about grace. First, no one can earn God's grace. Just as a gift is given — not earned — grace is extended to you through Jesus. It's not something you earn or deserve. Second, grace is free of charge. A gift is free to the recipient, but the giver bears the cost. In the same way, there is no way you can pay for God's grace. It is free of charge, even though it cost Jesus His life. Third, grace is secure. Once you have been given a gift, it belongs to you permanently. In the same way, the grace God gives you in Christ is forever yours; you cannot lose it, and no one can take it from you.

God offers you a gift, and that gift is His gracious favor. It's God's gracious favor that brings you into a relationship with Him through Jesus. It's God's gracious favor that sustains you each and every day. It's God's gracious favor that pours out blessings into your life and fills you with joy. It's God's gracious favor that equips and empowers you to serve God. And it is God's gracious favor that will preserve your life to the end and ultimately present you to the Father spotless and blameless.

From start to finish, your relationship with God is rooted completely in God's grace. This week we are going to be looking at God's grace and how you can grow in grace as you walk with Jesus.

THINK IT OUT

How do you define grace?

_____
_____
_____
_____
_____
_____

In what ways have you experienced God's grace in your life?

_____
_____
_____
_____
_____
_____
_____
_____

LIVE IT OUT

Begin memorizing your Scripture memory verse for the week:

*"For it is by grace you have been saved, through faith —
and this is not from yourselves, it is the gift of God —
not by works, so that no one can boast."*
(EPHESIANS 2.8-9 NIV)

Review your *"I Will"* statement for this week.

Read **(Luke 13:22-30)**. Continue to **l.i.s.t.e.n.** to God as you read and **p.r.a.y.**

PRAY IT OUT

Praise God and thank Him for His amazing grace in your life.
List specific things that God has done for you.

DAY ONE JOURNAL ENTRY

Look. **I**dentify. **S**tudy. **T**hink deeply. **E**ngage in prayer. **N**ote what God says.

_____
_____
_____
_____
_____
_____
_____
_____
_____
_____
_____
_____
_____
_____
_____
_____
_____
_____
_____
_____
_____
_____
_____
_____

Praise. **R**eturn. **A**sk. **Y**ield.

WEEK **SIX** · DAY **TWO**

GOD'S GRACE FOR SALVATION

One of the classic passages on God's saving grace is found in **(Ephesians 2.8-9 NIV)**, *"For it is by grace you have been saved, through faith — and this is not from yourselves, it is the gift of God — not by works, so that no one can boast."*

It is by grace you have been saved. God chose to extend His favor toward you through the death, burial and resurrection of Jesus Christ. At the point of believing in Jesus (faith), you stepped into the place of grace in which you now stand, **(Romans 5.2 ESV)**. That is an incredible reality. But before you can fully marvel at the wonder of God's grace, you must first understand your incredible and desperate need for God's grace.

A few verses earlier, Paul writes about our deplorable and hopeless condition, *"Once you were dead because of your disobedience and your many sins. You used to live in sin, just like the rest of the world, obeying the devil — the commander of the powers in the unseen world. He is the spirit at work in the hearts of those who refuse to obey God. All of us used to live that way, following the passionate desires and inclinations of our sinful nature. By our very nature we were subject to God's anger, just like everyone else,"* **(Ephesians 2.1-3 NLT)**.

This is a devastating picture of what we are like apart from God's grace. In other words, Paul is saying, *"before you came to Christ, you were dead in your sin, unresponsive, inattentive and unable to know God, reach out to Him or please Him. You lived in sin and embraced a sinful culture that was violating God at every turn, led by the devil himself, the ruler of the rebellious."*

Every one of us used to live this way — chasing our own desires and pleasures, allowing our wicked and wayward selves to run unleashed and unhindered — and in doing so we were objects of God's justice and wrath. This is an inconvenient truth. You don't deserve grace; no one does.

To those who feel that people are born naturally good, this is a punch in the gut. Paul writes, *"As the Scriptures say, 'No one is righteous — not even one. No one is truly wise; no one is seeking God. All have turned away; all have become useless. No one does good, not a single one',"* **(Romans 3.10-12 NLT)**.

Apart from Christ, you are not a friend of God; you are His enemy, **(Romans 5.10, 8.7; James 4.4 ESV)**. Sin is ultimate treason against your eternal King, and treason carries the stiff penalty of judgment and death, **(Romans 6.23 ESV)**. Until you fully grasp your terrible condition before God, you will never fully grasp the wonderful news of God's grace.

Paul continues, *"But because of his great love for us, God, who is rich in mercy, made us alive with Christ even when we were dead in transgressions — it is by grace you have been saved,"* **(Ephesians 2.4-5 NIV)**. When you deserved death, God chose to give you life. He chose to extend His favor, mercy and love toward those who did not deserve it and could not repay it.

That brings us back to our definition of grace – Grace is the undeserved gift of God's favor. When God sent Christ to pay your penalty, die your death and take your place on the cross, He was extending His grace. When He opened your eyes to truth, convicted your heart, drew you to Himself, covered your sin and made you a new person in Christ, He was extending His grace. When anyone comes to faith in Jesus, that person is justified by God's grace and now has the hope of eternal life, **(Titus 3.7 ESV)**.

God's grace stands in stark contrast to our own efforts to be right with God. No one can be right with God by being religious, fulfilling rituals or following rules. Any attempt in our own efforts to be good enough to come into God's presence is completely inadequate, **(Isaiah 64.6 ESV)**.

Paul states, *"For no one can ever be made right with God by doing what the law commands. The law simply shows us how sinful we are,"* **(Romans 3.20 NLT)**. God's law only shows us how incapable we are of fulfilling it and how desperate we are for God's mercy and favor.

After clearly seeing God's grace, one might ask, "Why would God decide to show us grace, especially when we have offended Him?" The answer is simply because God is full of grace. It is His nature and His choice and His desire to display His amazing grace. Joel declares, *"He is gracious and compassionate, slow to anger, abounding in lovingkindness and relenting of evil,"* **(Joel 2.13 NASB)**. Peter says that He is *"the God of all grace,"* **(1 Peter 5.10 ESV)**. John says that He is *"full of grace,"* **(John 1.14 ESV)** and **(Hebrews 10.29 ESV)** says that His Spirit is *"the Spirit of grace."* From beginning to end, your salvation was motivated and accomplished by God's grace.

THINK IT OUT

Why do you need God's grace in order to have a relationship with Him?

_____
_____
_____
_____
_____

Why does God choose to extend His grace?

_____
_____
_____
_____
_____
_____
_____
_____
_____

LIVE IT OUT

Review your memory verse for the week:

*"For it is by grace you have been saved, through faith —
and this is not from yourselves, it is the gift of God —
not by works, so that no one can boast."*
(EPHESIANS 2.8-9 NIV)

Review your *"I Will"* statement for this week.

Read **(Luke 14:1-14)**. Continue to **l.i.s.t.e.n.** to God as you read and **p.r.a.y.**

PRAY IT OUT

Thank God for salvation He has provided for you in Jesus.

DAY TWO JOURNAL ENTRY

Look. **I**dentify. **S**tudy. **T**hink deeply. **E**ngage in prayer. **N**ote what God says.

Praise. **R**eturn. **A**sk. **Y**ield.

WEEK **SIX** · DAY **THREE**

GOD'S GRACE WHEN I STRUGGLE

Following Jesus doesn't make you exempt from problems, trials and troubles. When you face those difficult days, what you need is God's grace to carry you through.

The Apostle Paul endured tremendous suffering during his lifetime. Because of his decision to follow Jesus, he was rejected, persecuted, beaten, shipwrecked and falsely accused. But those things didn't make Paul turn away from Jesus. In fact, quite the opposite was true. They drove him closer to Jesus.

Many people believe that Paul suffered from some kind of physical problem. Scholars can only guess what that problem may have been, but Paul knew that the Lord had allowed this affliction in his life for a reason. In **(2 Corinthians 12:8-9 NLT)** Paul wrote, *"Three different times I begged the Lord to take it away. Each time he said, 'My grace is all you need. My power works best in weakness'."* This was a low point in Paul's life. He was feeling discouraged and alone, but in Paul's pain, Jesus appeared to him and comforted him with these words, *"My grace is all you need."*

When you face your darkest moments, when you feel alone, only God's grace can pull you through. Instead of being angry with God or pushing Him away, Paul was happy to see that his troubles brought more of God's grace into his life. *"So now I am glad to boast about my weaknesses, so that the power of Christ can work through me. That's why I take pleasure in my weaknesses, and in the insults, hardships, persecutions, and troubles that I suffer for Christ. For when I am weak, then I am strong,"* **(2 Corinthians 12.9-10 NLT)**.

In your weakness, you can experience God's grace and strength. **(Hebrews 13.9 ESV)** says, *"It is good for the heart to be strengthened by grace, not by foods."* God's grace promises to strengthen you with all you need to face the troubles before you.

(2 Peter 3.18 ESV) says that as we trust the Lord in our troubles we *"grow in the grace and knowledge of our Lord and Savior Jesus Christ."* The more you trust Him in your troubles, the more you grow to rely on God's grace and the more you come to know Jesus deeply and personally.

How can you find grace and help when you need it most? Pray. **(Hebrews 4.16 NIV)** says, *"Let us then approach God's throne of grace with confidence, so that we may receive mercy and find grace to help us in our time of need."* When you come to the Lord Jesus in prayer, He promises to give you grace and help to overcome the problems you are facing.

You may ask, "*Why does God allow troubles to come into our lives anyway?*" While I cannot tell you specifically why you are facing certain problems, I do know that every problem gives you an opportunity to experience God's grace and trust Him more. Paul wrote to the church at Rome, *"Therefore, since we have been justified through faith, we have peace with God through our Lord Jesus Christ, through whom we have gained access by faith into this grace in which we now stand. And we boast in the hope of the glory of God. Not only so, but we also glory in our sufferings, because we know that suffering produces perseverance; perseverance, character; and character, hope. And hope does not put us to shame, because God's love has been poured out into our hearts through the Holy Spirit, who has been given to us,"* **(Romans 5.1-5 NIV)**.

Paul reminded them that because of Jesus, they were standing in the position of God's grace and favor. They were known and loved by God. Then he went on to describe why God allows troubles to come into our lives. Troubles give us the opportunity to trust the Lord and depend on His grace. When we do, we find that our troubles produce in us perseverance. We learn to keep our eyes on Jesus and follow Him no matter what. This perseverance produces godly character, and godly character produces hope because we know that God's promises are tried, tested and true. Through it all, we learn to experience the love of God through His Spirit.

Instead of troubles causing us to sink into despair, as we trust the Lord and rely on His grace, we are held up by a joy that only Jesus can give, **(James 1.2 ESV)**. This joy gives us hope that our troubles will not bring us down, but will ultimately make us stronger. Peter reminds us, *"And after you have suffered a little while, the God of all grace, who has called you to his eternal glory in Christ, will himself restore, confirm, strengthen, and establish you,"* **(1 Peter 5.10 ESV)**.

THINK IT OUT

What does God provide for us when we turn to Him with our problems?

_____
_____
_____
_____
_____

Why does God allow troubles to come into our lives?

_____
_____
_____
_____
_____

What is produced in us as we trust the Lord and depend on His grace?

_____
_____
_____
_____
_____

LIVE IT OUT

Review your Scripture memory verse for the week:

*"For it is by grace you have been saved, through faith —
and this is not from yourselves, it is the gift of God —
not by works, so that no one can boast."*
(EPHESIANS 2.8-9 NIV)

Review your *"I Will"* statement for this week.

Read **(Luke 15:11-32)**. Continue to **l.i.s.t.e.n.** to God as you read and **p.r.a.y.**

PRAY IT OUT

Ask God to help you with the troubles you are facing right now.

DAY THREE JOURNAL ENTRY

Look. **I**dentify. **S**tudy. **T**hink deeply. **E**ngage in prayer. **N**ote what God says.

Praise. **R**eturn. **A**sk. **Y**ield.

WEEK **SIX** · DAY **FOUR**

GOD'S GRACE WHEN I DOUBT

Many people deal with doubt. Sometimes we doubt God's goodness when troubles come our way. Other times, we struggle with doubt as we wrestle with the words of Jesus and what they mean for our lives today. For some, doubt is a huge obstacle that keeps them from moving forward in their walk with God. For others, doubt is a motivator to keep seeking, asking and searching for answers to their spiritual questions.

Overcoming doubt is part of every person's spiritual growth. If you have ever struggled with doubt, you are in good company. Many godly people have wrestled with doubt at some point in their lives.

Eve was in the Garden of Eden, enjoying all the goodness God had provided for her, and still she began to doubt God's promises, **(Genesis 3 ESV)**.

Zechariah, a faithful priest and righteous man, was told by an angel that his elderly wife would bear him a son, and he doubted, **(Luke 1.18-20 ESV)**.

John the Baptist, who was considered by Jesus to be the greatest man to ever live, struggled with doubt, **(Luke 7.18-19, 28 ESV)**.

Peter walked on water with Jesus, but seeing the wind and the waves, he doubted and sank, **(Matthew 14.31 ESV)**.

Even Jesus' own disciples struggled with doubt from time to time, **(Matthew 28.17 ESV)**, and Thomas, one of the twelve apostles, struggled so much that he was later referred to as *"doubting Thomas,"* **(John 20.24-29 ESV)**.

There are other great men and women in the Bible who had doubts. People like Abraham, Moses, Isaac, Jacob, Job and David. The list could go on of people who wrestled with doubt at some point in their lives.

There are some misconceptions about doubt. Some think doubt and unbelief are the same thing, but they are different. Unbelief is the refusal to accept what God has said. Doubt is struggling to trust God completely in some area of your life. Some think doubt is unforgivable, but it isn't. As I just pointed out, many godly people — both past and present — have wrestled with doubt from time to time. Some think doubt is permanent, but it isn't. God can move you from doubt to great confidence in Him, just as He has done for many people.

Before we go any further, let me warn you that persistent doubt can have very devastating effects. Doubt can keep you from experiencing God's power, receiving God's promises, experiencing God's presence, enjoying God's blessing and embracing God's purpose for your life. In **(James 1.5-8 ESV)**, we're essentially informed, *"that if we persist in doubt, our prayers won't be effective and we won't receive all that God wants to give us."*

Behind it all is Satan's plan to erode our confidence in God and keep us from enjoying all that God has for us. The remedy for doubt is rock-solid faith. The more you confidently trust God, the less you doubt Him. In fact, faith is essential to your walk with God. **(Hebrews 11.6 ESV)** says, *"And without faith it is impossible to please him."* You can't really know God deeply, experience His power or rely on His promises unless you confidently trust Him.

So, how do you move from persistent doubt to resolute faith? You may be like the desperate father described in **(Mark 9.22-24 NIV)** who brought his son to Jesus and said, *"But if you can do anything, take pity on us and help us. 'If you can?' said Jesus. 'Everything is possible for the one who believes.'"* Startled by his own doubt, the father cried out, *"I do believe; help me overcome my unbelief!"*

You may be praying that same thing, *"Lord, I do believe you, but help me overcome my doubt!"* Looking back on how Jesus helped John the Baptist overcome his own doubts, we learn some great lessons... see **(Luke 7.18-23 ESV)**. First, John verbalized his doubts. He was questioning whether Jesus was truly the Messiah. His questions and doubts were only strengthened by the fact that John was in a dark and difficult place in his life. He had been thrown into prison and was struggling with discouragement. In his struggle, John verbalized his questions to his friends. Often doubts rise when troubles come. Instead of holding in your doubts and struggles, verbalize them to trusted godly friends who can help you.

Second, Jesus pointed John back to God's Word. In **(Luke 7.22 NIV)** Jesus tells John's disciples to go back and report that *"the blind receive sight, the lame walk, those who have leprosy are cleansed, the deaf hear, the dead are raised, and the good news is proclaimed to the poor."* Here Jesus is referring to **(Isaiah 61.1-2 ESV)**, which states that when the Messiah comes, He will do all these things. **(Romans 10.17 ESV)** says, *"So faith comes from hearing, and hearing through the word of Christ."*

At least twice, the Word of God is called the *"word of his grace,"* **(Acts 14.3, 20.32 ESV)**. That is, God uses His Word to bring grace and favor and help when we need it most, especially in seasons of doubt. Saturate your mind with God's Word. Put your whole weight down on God's promise. Go back to the truths that you have become convinced of and the people who told these truths to you, **(2 Timothy 3.14-15 ESV)**.

Third, look at what God has done. Jesus pointed John to evidence of God's work — people's lives were being transformed. Look to the past and remember what God has done for you. Look around and see the handiwork of God in creation. Look at the lives of others who have trusted the Lord and seen Him work in their lives. **(Psalm 77.11 NIV)** says, *"I will remember the deeds of the LORD; yes, I will remember your miracles of long ago."*

Fourth, eventually John took his doubts to Jesus. Only Jesus could ease his mind and clear away his doubts. Ask Jesus to give you great faith, **(Romans 12.3 ESV)**. Ask Jesus to give you grace to overcome the doubts you are facing. **(James 4.6 ESV)** says, *"God … gives grace to the humble."*

Even in seasons of doubt, God gives His grace to move you toward greater confidence in Him. I believe Jesus ultimately gave John the grace to endure and overcome his doubts, and I know He will do the same for you. **(John 1.15-17 ESV)** says, *"John [the Baptist] bore witness about him, and cried out, This was he of whom I said, 'He who comes after me ranks before me, because he was before me.' From his fullness we have all received, grace upon grace."*

THINK IT OUT

Describe a time when you wrestled with doubt?

_____
_____
_____
_____
_____
_____
_____

What can you do to overcome doubt in your life?

_____
_____
_____
_____
_____

What stood out most to you about this study on overcoming doubt?

___

LIVE IT OUT

Review your Scripture memory verse for the week:

*"For it is by grace you have been saved, through faith —
and this is not from yourselves, it is the gift of God —
not by works, so that no one can boast."*
(EPHESIANS 2.8-9 NIV)

Review your *"I Will"* statement for this week.

Read **(Luke 16:19-31)**. Continue to **l.i.s.t.e.n.** to God as you read and **p.r.a.y.**

PRAY IT OUT

Confess to God the areas where you doubt His goodness.

DAY FOUR JOURNAL ENTRY

Look. Identify. Study. Think deeply. Engage in prayer. Note what God says.

Praise. Return. Ask. Yield.

WEEK **SIX** · DAY **FIVE**

GOD'S GRACE WHEN I FAIL

Everyone fails. No one is perfect except Jesus. Even when you are walking with God and doing all you know to do to please Him, there will still be times when you give in to temptation and you fall into sin. What do you do then? That is when you run toward God's grace.

The Apostle Paul was explaining God's grace to the church in Rome. In Romans 5, he contrasts Adam's sin that brought sin into the world with Jesus' death that brought forgiveness and grace to us. *"Yes, Adam's one sin brings condemnation for everyone, but Christ's one act of righteousness brings a right relationship with God and new life for everyone. Because one person disobeyed God, many became sinners. But because one other person obeyed God, many will be made righteous. God's law was given so that all people could see how sinful they were. But as people sinned more and more, God's wonderful grace became more abundant. So just as sin ruled over all people and brought them to death, now God's wonderful grace rules instead, giving us right standing with God and resulting in eternal life through Jesus Christ our Lord,"* **(Romans 5.18-21 NLT)**.

Paul was making the case that even though sin is now part of the world and separates us from God, His grace reaches the distances and can bring us back into fellowship with Him. God's grace is able to cover our sin and restore us. No matter how deep the sin, God's grace is deeper still! There is nothing you can do that is outside the reach of God's grace and forgiveness.

Jesus demonstrated God's grace throughout His ministry. He spent His time reaching out to the outcast and the marginalized. One day a group of religious leaders was criticizing Him for this and Jesus responded, *"It is not the healthy who need a doctor, but the sick. I have not come to call the righteous, but sinners,"* **(Mark 2.17 NIV)**. Jesus knew that every person mattered to the Father, and no one was out of reach of His grace.

How should we respond when we fail and find ourselves in need of God's grace? **(1 John 1.9 NIV)** says, *"If we confess our sins, he is faithful and just and will forgive us our sins and purify us from all unrighteousness."* God expects us to turn to Him when we sin and confess it quickly. Confess means to agree with God that what we did was wrong and sinful before Him. You should never minimize your sin, excuse it or shift the blame to others. Instead, you should readily confess it to God. **(Proverbs 28.13 NLT)** says, *"People who conceal their sins will not prosper, but if they confess and turn from them, they will receive mercy."* When you turn to God and confess your sin to Him, He will forgive you, clean you and restore your fellowship with Him, **(Hebrews 10.17; Psalm 103.10-12 ESV)**.

Now some have thought, *"Well, if God's grace is greater than my sin, then the more I sin, the more grace I get!"* This thinking has led some people to dive headlong into sinful living. But this isn't at all what God wants for you. Keep reading. *"Well then, should we keep on sinning so that God can show us more and more of his wonderful grace? Of course not! Since we have died to sin, how can we continue to live in it? Or have you forgotten that when we were joined with Christ Jesus in baptism, we joined him in his death? For we died and were buried with Christ by baptism. And just as Christ was raised from the dead by the glorious power of the Father, now we also may live new lives,"* **(Romans 6.1-4 NLT)**.

Paul is saying that we should never take for granted God's grace by willfully sinning. Instead, because of God's grace and the change He has made in our lives, we should avoid sin altogether. How can we keep doing what we used to do before we came to Christ? If our old life is dead in Christ, how can we act like we are still the same old person we used to be?

No, grace doesn't lead you to sin. In fact, grace teaches you to say no to sin and to live like Jesus. **(Titus 2.11-14 NIV)** says, *"For the grace of God has appeared that offers salvation to all people. It teaches us to say 'No' to ungodliness and worldly passions, and to live self-controlled, upright and godly lives in this present age, while we wait for the blessed hope — the appearing of the glory of our great God and Savior, Jesus Christ, who gave himself for us to redeem us from all wickedness and to purify for himself a people that are his very own, eager to do what is good."*

God's grace reminds us and motivates us to live differently than the world, because we are looking forward to Jesus' return. He has redeemed you — literally bought you back with His own blood on the cross — from your old way of life, and now is making you His very own — forgiven, clean and eager to do what pleases Him. It is God's grace that empowers obedience, and obedience is what produces holy living.

THINK IT OUT

What does God's Word say about His grace and your sin?

___
___
___
___
___
___
___

How should you respond when you sin against God?

How does God's grace teach you to live today?

LIVE IT OUT

Review your Scripture memory verse for the week:

*"For it is by grace you have been saved, through faith —
and this is not from yourselves, it is the gift of God —
not by works, so that no one can boast."*
(EPHESIANS 2.8-9 NIV)

Review your *"I Will"* statement for this week.

Read **(Luke 17:11-19)**. Continue to **l.i.s.t.e.n.** to God as you read and **p.r.a.y.**

PRAY IT OUT

Praise God that His grace covers you when you fail.

DAY FIVE JOURNAL ENTRY

Look. **I**dentify. **S**tudy. **T**hink deeply. **E**ngage in prayer. **N**ote what God says.

Praise. **R**eturn. **A**sk. **Y**ield.

WEEK **SIX** · DAY **SIX**

EXTENDING GOD'S GRACE TO OTHERS

Each of us stands in need of God's grace, but each of us also has the opportunity to reflect God's grace to the people around us. **(2 Corinthians 3.18 TLB)** says, *"We can be mirrors that brightly reflect the glory of the Lord. And as the Spirit of the Lord works with us, we become more and more like him."*

As the Spirit of God continues to transform you on the inside, you become more and more like Jesus, and you begin to reflect Him to those around you. Part of what we reflect to others is the grace of God. Jesus told His disciples, *"Freely you have received; freely give,"* **(Matthew 10.8 NIV)**. Just as you have received the gracious favor of God, now let God use you to show His grace to others.

You may ask, *"How can I show God's grace to my family, friends, co-workers or even strangers?"*

Here are some practical ways:

Extend forgiveness.
"In him we have redemption through his blood, the forgiveness of sins, in accordance with the riches of God's grace," **(Ephesians 1.7 NIV)**. The grace of God through the sacrifice of Jesus forgives your sin and restores your relationship with God. One way you can extend God's grace to others is by forgiving those who have offended you. In that way, your life becomes a living portrait of the gospel. In fact, Jesus said that *"if you do not forgive others their sins, your Father will not forgive your sins,"* **(Matthew 6.15 NIV)**. Receiving God's grace and forgiveness requires that you extend God's grace and forgiveness to others. After reminding the church in Ephesus about the grace they received, the Apostle Paul added, *"Be kind and compassionate to one another, forgiving each other, just as in Christ God forgave you,"* **(Ephesians 4.32 NIV)**. Just as Jesus forgave you, forgive others. Just as Jesus was gracious toward you, be gracious toward others. This way, you put God's grace on display for the world to see.

Extend encouragement.
(Colossians 4.6 NIV) says, *"Let your conversation be always full of grace, seasoned with salt, so that you may know how to answer everyone."* Another way we can extend God's grace is by the words we choose. Gracious words are life giving. They point to Jesus. They are seasoned with truth

and kindness. *"Do not let any unwholesome talk come out of your mouths, but only what is helpful for building others up according to their needs, that it may benefit those who listen,"* **(Ephesians 4.29 NIV)**. The opposite of gracious words are *"unwholesome"* words. The term can be translated *"abusive, corrupt"* — it literally means *"rotten or worthless."* Worthless words inflict pain; gracious words bring healing. Worthless words are abusive; gracious words are gentle. Worthless words tear down; gracious words build up. Worthless words injure; gracious words benefit those who hear them.

Extend a helping hand.
"In his grace, God has given us different gifts for doing certain things well," **(Romans 12.6 NLT)**. You can extend God's grace by serving people with the talents and gifts God has given you. At your birth, God instilled in you certain aptitudes and abilities as part of the fabric of your unique design. At your rebirth, the Spirit also gifted you with certain spiritual gifts, energizing you with His power to serve others and glorify God. When you serve other people using the talents and gifts God has given you, you are extending grace to them. Peter wrote, *"Each of you should use whatever gift you have received to serve others, as faithful stewards of God's grace in its various forms,"* **(I Peter 4.10 NIV)**. In a sense, you are a steward of God's gifts. They are yours on loan from God, and you are accountable to Him for how you use what He gave you to serve others. I'm sure in God's eyes, it is a beautiful picture to see His people receiving His grace through special gifts and then sharing them with others. The result is that grace is multiplied and joy grows exponentially.

Extend the hope of the gospel.
The Apostle Paul never got over the grace that God showed him. In **(1 Timothy 1.13-16 NIV)** he wrote to his young ministry apprentice, Timothy, *"Even though I was once a blasphemer and a persecutor and a violent man, I was shown mercy because I acted in ignorance and unbelief. The grace of our Lord was poured out on me abundantly, along with the faith and love that are in Christ Jesus. Here is a trustworthy saying that deserves full acceptance: Christ Jesus came into the world to save sinners — of whom I am the worst. But for that very reason I was shown mercy so that in me, the worst of sinners, Christ Jesus might display his immense patience as an example for those who would believe in him and receive eternal life."*

In other words, Paul was saying: *"I was the worst guy you could imagine ... and yet God chose to pour His grace on me full to overflowing! If I can be saved, anyone can be saved!"* Paul was so overwhelmed with God's grace in his life that he was compelled to share that good news with other people. In **(1 Corinthians 9.16 NIV)** Paul said, *"For when I preach the gospel, I cannot boast, since I am compelled to preach. Woe to me if I do not preach the gospel!"* In **(Ephesians 3.2 NIV)**, He described the gospel as *"the administration of God's grace,"* that was given to him to pass on to others. One of the ways you can extend God's grace to others is simply by telling them what Jesus has done for you, and how they can come to know Him personally. There is no greater reward than sharing the gospel with people who desperately need God's grace.

THINK IT OUT

Which one of these four ways to extend grace stands out to you?

How could you begin to extend God's grace to your family?

Which one of these would be the most difficult for you?

_____
_____
_____
_____
_____
_____
_____
_____

LIVE IT OUT

Review your Scripture memory verse for the week:

*"For it is by grace you have been saved, through faith —
and this is not from yourselves, it is the gift of God —
not by works, so that no one can boast."*
(EPHESIANS 2.8-9 NIV)

Review your *"I Will"* statement for this week.

Read **(Luke 18:9-14)**. Continue to **l.i.s.t.e.n.** to God as you read and **p.r.a.y.**

PRAY IT OUT

Pray specifically for those in your life that need to experience God's grace.
Ask Him to use you to show them His grace.

DAY SIX JOURNAL ENTRY

Look. Identify. Study. Think deeply. Engage in prayer. Note what God says.

Praise. Return. Ask. Yield.

WEEK **SIX** · DAY **SEVEN**

EMBRACE GRACE

Grace is not just a one-time experience; it is a daily reality for the follower of Jesus. **(John 1.16 ESV)** says, **"For from his fullness we have all received grace upon grace."** Like the tide that continually rolls in wave after wave, never stopping, never ending; God's grace is always moving toward you, day after day, moment by moment.

There is a beautiful picture of God's grace found in the Book of 2 Samuel. After finally subduing his enemies, King David was living in his palace in Jerusalem. One day, the Lord put on his heart to extend grace to the household of his best friend, Jonathan, who had died in a bloody battle against the Philistines. David inquired if there were any of Jonathan's children still alive that he could bless.

It was reported that Jonathan's youngest son, Mephibosheth, was alive and living in a small remote village in Israel. Mephibosheth was only five years old when his father died, and when the word of the tragedy reached Jonathan's home, his family panicked and fled. In the process, the young woman carrying Mephibosheth tripped and fell, permanently crippling him in both feet. In every way, this young man was completely unable to care for himself. Twice in the chapter it is reported that he was *"lame in both feet,"* **(2 Samuel 9.3,13 NIV)**.

David summoned Mephibosheth to his palace and he said, *"Don't be afraid ... for I will surely show you kindness for the sake of your father Jonathan. I will restore to you all the land that belonged to your grandfather Saul, and you will always eat at my table,"* **(2 Samuel 9.7 NIV)**. Now this is a picture of grace! David was saying, *"Because of my love for your father, I will treat you as one of my own. I will restore to you all the property that belonged to your grandfather, King Saul, and you will live with me and enjoy my fellowship at my table all the days of your life!"* This is over-the-top, head-shaking, shoulder-shrugging, unbelievable grace. While most kings would have seen an heir to the throne as an enemy to be annihilated, David chose to set his grace and kindness upon Mephibosheth because of his relationship with Jonathan.

What David did that day was truly an undeserved gift of favor. This is what God the Father has done for you and me. While we were enemies of God, rebels and lawbreakers, God chose to set His affection and kindness on us — not because of anything we have done, but because of His Son, Jesus. We are loved because of Jesus. We are accepted because of Jesus. We are blessed because of Jesus. Now, we are a part of God's family, citizens of heaven, promised a new home with Him forever and enjoying fellowship with the Father — all because of Jesus.

What is the proper response to such lavish grace? Fully embrace God's grace in your life every day.

How can you embrace God's grace? First, realize that your position of favor before God is not a result of your own work or efforts, but solely because of Jesus. In **(Ephesians 1.3-10 NIV)**, the Apostle Paul wrote: *"Praise be to the God and Father of our Lord Jesus Christ, who has blessed us in the heavenly realms with every spiritual blessing in Christ. For he chose us in him before the creation of the world to be holy and blameless in his sight. In love he predestined us for adoption to sonship through Jesus Christ, in accordance with his pleasure and will — to the praise of his glorious grace, which he has freely given us in the One he loves. In him we have redemption through his blood, the forgiveness of sins, in accordance with the riches of God's grace that he lavished on us. With all wisdom and understanding, he made known to us the mystery of his will according to his good pleasure, which he purposed in Christ, to be put into effect when the times reach their fulfillment — to bring unity to all things in heaven and on earth under Christ."*

Here Paul is listing off some of the blessings that are ours because of God's grace. Notice the phrases in Him or in Christ, or through Jesus Christ. The fact that you are forgiven, adopted, chosen, clean, loved and drawn near to God, coupled with the fact that you have been given joy, hope, peace, assurance, power and favor — all of this is because of what Jesus accomplished on the cross.

Don't ever think that somehow you have earned your place at God's table because of the good things you have done. Don't ever think that God had mercy on you because you tried to live a moral life or did your best to be a good person. The only reason you have experienced the grace of God is because of Jesus. The Father showered grace on you on behalf of His Son.

Because you didn't earn your seat at the table of God's favor, there is nothing you can do to maintain your place of grace. Mephibosheth did not do anything to deserve David's blessings and nothing was required of him to maintain them. In the same way, just as you came into a relationship with God by grace, now live every day depending and relying on His grace.

Another way to embrace God's grace in your daily life is to be thankful for all God has done for you. When King David announced all he planned to do for him, *"Mephibosheth bowed down and said, 'What is your servant, that you should notice a dead dog like me?,'"* **(2 Samuel 9.8 NIV)**. He realized how unworthy he was to receive such grace. I can imagine every time Mephibosheth woke up in the palace, he was reminded of how blessed he was to be there. One minute he was an enemy of the king, hiding out in a small village. The next minute, he was treated as a son of the King, eating at his table.

Paul wrote, *"Praise be to the God and Father of our Lord Jesus Christ, who has blessed us in the heavenly realms with every spiritual blessing in Christ,"* **(Ephesians 1.3 NIV)**. This is why we praise Jesus. This is why we worship Him. Because His steadfast love never fails. **(Psalm 107.1 NIV)** says, *"Give thanks to the LORD, for he is good; his love endures forever."* Choose to live every day with gratitude in your heart. Remember that every good thing that comes into your life is an expression of God's love and grace toward you, **(James 1.17 ESV)**.

Jesus modeled this for us. During His last meal with His disciples, Jesus prayed, *"Now they know that everything you have given me comes from you,"* **(John 17.7 NIV)**. Jesus knew that every good thing, every blessing, every success, came from His Father. Never begin to think that the blessings you have on this earth are because of your hard work or wise planning. All that you enjoy are blessings from God, who loves to shower you with His grace.

A third way to embrace God's grace in your life is to be loyal to King Jesus. Serve Him, love Him and obey Him. Mephibosheth's loyalty would later be tested, but he doggedly refused to turn against his king. The best response to God's grace is to live your life for Jesus unashamed and unreserved. **(Romans 12.1-2 NIV)** says, *"Therefore, I urge you, brothers and sisters, in view of God's mercy, to offer your bodies as a living sacrifice, holy and pleasing to God — this is your true and proper worship. Do not conform to the pattern of this world, but be transformed by the renewing of your mind. Then you will be able to test and approve what God's will is — his good, pleasing and perfect will."* Paul was saying, *"in view of God's mercy, offer your body."*

In light of God's grace, the only proper response is obedience to Jesus. Be loyal to your King. Don't conform to this world. Allow God's Word to transform you completely. Seek to know and do His perfect will for your life, but remember that even your obedience is an expression of God's grace. In **(Philippians 2.12-13 NIV)** Paul wrote, *"Continue to work out your salvation with fear and trembling, for it is God who works in you to will and to act in order to fulfill his good purpose."* Even your desire and ability to obey Jesus comes from your heavenly Father. It's all God's grace from start to finish.

Finally, you can embrace God's grace daily by sharing with others what God has done for you. As one old preacher used to say, *"I'm just one beggar telling another beggar where he got some bread."* When you share with others how God has poured His grace and forgiveness into your life, you glorify God and put His grace on display for all to see, **(Ephesians 1.6 ESV)**.

THINK IT OUT

What is your reaction to the story of Mephibosheth?

_____
_____
_____
_____
_____
_____

How can you embrace God's grace in your life?

___

LIVE IT OUT

Review your Scripture memory verse for the week:

*"For it is by grace you have been saved, through faith —
and this is not from yourselves, it is the gift of God —
not by works, so that no one can boast."*
(EPHESIANS 2.8-9 NIV)

Review your *"I Will"* statement for this week.

Take the day to review the notes you made through your reading in Luke.
Reflect on what God has spoken to you.

PRAY IT OUT

Praise God that He has shown you His favor in so many ways.

FOR GROUP TIME

My "I Will" Statement:

As a result of what I have just studied, I will put this one thing into practice this week:

DAY SEVEN JOURNAL ENTRY

Look. **I**dentify. **S**tudy. **T**hink deeply. **E**ngage in prayer. **N**ote what God says.

Praise. **R**eturn. **A**sk. **Y**ield.

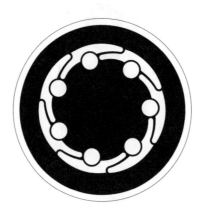

CONNECTING WITH GOD'S FAMILY

WEEK SEVEN

▶ **MEMORY VERSE**

"... you are no longer foreigners and strangers, but fellow citizens with God's people and also members of his household..."

(EPHESIANS 2.19 NIV)

WEEK **SEVEN** · DAY **ONE**

CREATED FOR COMMUNITY

The National Science Foundation conducted an extensive research project on loneliness in America. The findings were highlighted in the *"American Sociological Review."* After interviewing over 1,500 people — all face to face — researchers reported that one out of four Americans said they had *"no one with whom they could talk about their personal troubles or triumphs."* Also, more than half of those interviewed said they had *"no one to talk to beyond their immediate family."* This led researchers to conclude that there is growing *"social isolation"* in our country. Does that surprise you?

If these findings are true, then the next question is, *"Why?"* Why are we so desperate for relationships? Why do we need community so badly? Why are we wired this way?

The answer to the *"Why?"* question is found in the Bible. The reason community and healthy relationships matter so much is because you were created for community. You were created to know and be known, love and be loved, care and be cared for, celebrate and be celebrated. The Bible tells us that *"God exists in community, one God existing in three persons: the Father, the Son and the Holy Spirit."* We see all three of them at work in creation.

"In the beginning, God created the heavens and the earth. The earth was without form and void, and darkness was over the face of the deep. And the Spirit of God was hovering over the face of the waters. And God said, 'Let there be light,' and there was light," **(Genesis 1.1-3 ESV)**. In this passage, we see God the Father as the grand designer. He conceived the heavens and the earth, bringing them into being. We see God the Spirit hovering over the face of the waters, not so much creating, but watching over until the creation reaches its desired completion. Then we see the spoken word — *"Let there be light,"* and the Word brings into being what the Father has in mind.

Later, in the Book of John we read, *"In the beginning was the Word, and the Word was with God and the Word was God. ... And the Word became flesh and dwelt among us,"* **(John 1.1,14 ESV)**. The Word is Jesus. It is through Jesus that the world came into being, **(Colossians 1.15-16 ESV)**. Right from the beginning, we learn that God exists in community. There was never a time when God did not know and enjoy community. It's His nature. It's who He is.

After creating the world, God created man *"in his own image,"* **(Genesis 1.27 ESV)**. This means that we were created as His image bearers, and with that, comes our capacity and desire for community. You could say you have His *"relational DNA"* flowing through you.

After everything was created, God saw that it all was *"good"*! But there was one thing that was not good. **Then the LORD God said, "It is not good that the man should be alone; I will make him a helper fit for him," (Genesis 2.18 ESV)**. It was not good for man to live alone, so God created the first woman. He provided community.

This statement is not as much about marriage as it is about relationships. It is not good for people to live in isolation. When we do, we ache. While we were created for community, that community was lost because of sin. Sin divided what God created to be together. But through the cross, Jesus came to restore what was broken. In Christ, our relationship with God is restored, and in Christ, we are brought into a new community with one another. That new community is found in the church. This week we are going to look at the important role the church has in God's plan for your life.

THINK IT OUT

Do you sense that we are experiencing a culture of *"social isolation"*? Why?

_____
_____
_____
_____
_____
_____
_____
_____
_____
_____

How do you cultivate healthy community in your life?

___

LIVE IT OUT

Begin memorizing the Scripture memory verse for the week:

"You are no longer foreigners and strangers, but fellow citizens with God's people and also members of his household."
(EPHESIANS 2.19, NIV)

Review your *"I Will"* statement for this week.

Read **(Luke 19:28-44)**. Continue to **l.i.s.t.e.n.** to God as you read and **p.r.a.y.**

PRAY IT OUT

Take time to Praise God today that He made you with the need and capacity for community. Ask Him to bring good friends into your life.

DAY ONE JOURNAL ENTRY

Look. **I**dentify. **S**tudy. **T**hink deeply. **E**ngage in prayer. **N**ote what God says.

Praise. **R**eturn. **A**sk. **Y**ield.

WEEK **SEVEN** · DAY **TWO**

WELCOME TO THE FAMILY

The gospel is not only about believing, it is also about belonging. When someone comes to faith in Jesus, that person becomes part of the church. To follow Jesus means to be part of His church. It would have been strange and unthinkable in the New Testament for a person to claim to follow Jesus and not be part of God's new community, the church.

So, what is the church? Is it just steeples and traditions — just buildings and rituals? Throughout all times and cultures, the church is defined as baptized believers who are saved by faith in Jesus Christ. The Bible tells us that Jesus loves the church and gave Himself up for her, **(Ephesians 5.25 ESV)**. Jesus is the head of the church, **(Ephesians 5.22-23 ESV)**, and Jesus is actively building His church, **(Matthew 16.18 ESV)**. Even the growth of the church is something that God does by His Spirit, **(Acts 2.47 ESV)**.

In one sense, the church is universal, encompassing all believers of all times. In another sense, the church is local, as believers gather together to worship Jesus and carry out His mission. The Scriptures give us many metaphors or word pictures to describe the church. The church is called the bride of Christ. Husbands are to love their wives in the same way Jesus loves His church and gave Himself up for her, **(Ephesians 5.25 ESV)**. The church is called a family, where we have one heavenly Father. Jesus is our older brother, and we are brothers and sisters in him, **(Romans 8.16-17; Ephesians 3.14-15; 2 Corinthians 6.18 ESV)**. The church is called a building where Jesus is the cornerstone, and we are fitted together like stones to make a new temple where God is worshiped and praised, **(1 Peter 2.4-8 ESV)**.

However, the church is most often called the body of Christ. Your physical body is made up of many different parts, each doing its designed job to make the body function. Likewise, when believers get together and serve in their unique skills and talents, we work together to reflect Jesus and become the tangible expression of His ministry in the world, **(1 Corinthians 12.12-27 ESV)**. In this picture, Jesus is the head of the church, **(Ephesians 4.15-16 ESV)**.

Being part of the church reminds us that we are part of something bigger than ourselves. As followers of Jesus, we are part of a larger community of faith that stretches through time, across cultures and around the world. That is why we are encouraged to gather with the church as fully participating members. **(Hebrews 10.25 NLT)** warns, *"And let us not neglect our meeting together, as some people do, but encourage one another, especially now that the day of his return is drawing near."*

THINK IT OUT

How would you define the church?

_____
_____
_____
_____
_____
_____
_____
_____

What has been your church experience?

_____
_____
_____
_____
_____
_____
_____
_____

Are you a participating member of a local church? If not, why not?

___

LIVE IT OUT

Review your Scripture memory verse for the week:

"You are no longer foreigners and strangers, but fellow citizens with God's people and also members of his household."
(EPHESIANS 2.19 NIV)

Review your *"I Will"* statement for this week.

Read **(Luke 20:9-19)**. Continue to **l.i.s.t.e.n.** to God as you read and **p.r.a.y.**

PRAY IT OUT

Thank God that He created the church to be a place of community for you.

DAY TWO JOURNAL ENTRY

Look. **I**dentify. **S**tudy. **T**hink deeply. **E**ngage in prayer. **N**ote what God says.

Praise. **R**eturn. **A**sk. **Y**ield.

WEEK **SEVEN** · DAY **THREE**

BAPTISM

When anyone comes to faith in Jesus, there is a huge celebration! When my girls were born, we celebrated each new birth. In the same way, when a person is born again into God's family, **(John 3.3 ESV)**, all of heaven celebrates, **(Luke 15.7 ESV)**. The church also celebrates when a person comes to Christ, and part of that celebration is through baptism.

Baptism was so important to Jesus that He was baptized Himself, leaving us an example to follow, **(Matthew 3.13-15 ESV)**. He also commanded His followers to be baptized, **(Matthew 28.19 ESV)**. Throughout church history, there have been many views on baptism, so let's look at God's Word to answer five key questions:

What is baptism? The word baptism comes from the Greek word *baptizo* meaning *"to dip, plunge or immerse."* The early church used baptism to picture the death, burial and resurrection of Jesus and to identify the new believer as a follower of Jesus and part of the church. *"For you were buried with Christ when you were baptized. And with him you were raised to new life because you trusted the mighty power of God, who raised Christ from the dead,"* **(Colossians 2.12 NLT)**.

Who can be baptized? Baptism is the outward declaration of faith in Jesus; therefore, only those who have repented of their sin and believed in Jesus in saving faith should be baptized. *"Peter replied, 'Each of you must repent of your sins and turn to God, and be baptized in the name of Jesus Christ for the forgiveness of your sins,'"* **(Acts 2.38 NLT)**. There is no evidence in Scripture of a person being baptized without first being a believer in Jesus.

When can a person be baptized? A person can be baptized after he or she professes faith in Jesus. Philip explained the gospel to an Ethiopian official, and after receiving Christ, he was immediately baptized, **(Acts 8.36-38 ESV)**.

How should a person be baptized? Biblical baptism is by immersion in water. As previously noted, the Greek word *baptizo* means *"to immerse."* When Scripture describes Jesus' baptism, it says He came up out of the water. *"As Jesus came up out of the water, he saw the heavens splitting apart and the Holy Spirit descending on him like a dove,"* **(Mark 1.10 NLT)**. Immersion is the only method that clearly portrays the death, burial and resurrection of Jesus.

Why should a person be baptized? A believer should be baptized out of obedience to Jesus, who commanded us to be baptized, **(Matthew 28.19 ESV)**. Baptism is often called the *"first step of obedience"* to Jesus. We should also be baptized as a way of publicly professing our faith in Jesus Christ. However, baptism is never a requirement for salvation. In **(Titus 3.4-6 NLT)** Paul wrote, *"When God our Savior revealed his kindness and love, he saved us, not because of the righteous things we had done, but because of his mercy. He washed away our sins, giving us a new birth and new life through the Holy Spirit. He generously poured out the Spirit upon us through Jesus Christ our Savior."*

Baptism is a wonderful celebration of what Jesus has done and the grace He has shown in our lives.

THINK IT OUT

What does baptism mean?

_____
_____
_____
_____
_____
_____
_____
_____

Why should a person be baptized?

_____
_____
_____
_____
_____

Were you baptized after your profession of faith in Jesus? If so, please explain what happened.

_____
_____
_____
_____
_____
_____
_____
_____

LIVE IT OUT

Review your Scripture memory verse for the week:

"You are no longer foreigners and strangers, but fellow citizens with God's people and also members of his household."
(EPHESIANS 2.19 NIV)

Review your *"I Will"* statement for this week.

Read **(Luke 21:5-19)**. Continue to **l.i.s.t.e.n.** to God as you read and **p.r.a.y.**

PRAY IT OUT

Take time to remember your baptism and what the moment meant to you. Thank Him for His grace in your life. If you have not been baptized since you came to know and follow Jesus, ask God to give you courage to obey Him in this area.

DAY THREE JOURNAL ENTRY

Look. **I**dentify. **S**tudy. **T**hink deeply. **E**ngage in prayer. **N**ote what God says.

Praise. **R**eturn. **A**sk. **Y**ield.

WEEK **SEVEN** · DAY **FOUR**

A PLACE OF WORSHIP

Church is a place to worship. Whenever believers gather together — whether it's in a church building or in a park — one of the central reasons they come together is to worship God.

You may ask, *"What does it really mean to worship? And what is the church's role in worshiping God?"* Worship starts in heaven. God is awesome and holy, and He alone deserves worship and praise. The Bible says that angels worship God at all times, crying out, *"Holy, Holy, Holy is the LORD Almighty; the whole earth is full of His glory,"* **(Isaiah 6.3 NIV);** also **(Revelation 4.8-11, 11.17-18 ESV)**.

God also is looking for worshipers on earth who will exalt His name and praise Him. Jesus said, *"Yet a time is coming and has now come when the true worshipers will worship the Father in the Spirit and in truth, for they are the kind of worshipers the Father seeks. God is spirit, and his worshipers must worship in the Spirit and in truth,"* **(John 4.23-24 NIV)**. God is actively looking for worshipers whose hearts are fully devoted to Him, **(2 Chronicles 16.9 ESV)**, and who will worship Him in light of the truth revealed in Jesus Christ, **(John 14.6 ESV)**.

Followers of Jesus Christ have every reason to worship God. He has saved us, adopted us, forgiven us and redeemed us — we have every reason to praise Him. In fact, everyone is wired for worship. We were created to give our praise, admiration, affection and attention to something. We will either give our worship to temporal things like idols, cash, possessions, sports and people, or we will give our hearts in worship to the God who created us and loves us. When believers gather together, they gather to worship. While God desires that we also worship Him privately, there is something special that happens when believers come together in community to worship God.

What does "gathered" worship look like?

We worship through music. *"Come, let us sing to the LORD! Let us shout joyfully to the Rock of our salvation. Let us come to him with thanksgiving. Let us sing psalms of praise to him. For the LORD is a great God, a great King above all gods,"* **(Psalm 95.1-3 NLT)**.

We worship through giving. *"Each of you should give what you have decided in your heart to give, not reluctantly or under compulsion, for God loves a cheerful giver,"* **(2 Corinthians 9.7 NIV)**.

We worship through serving God and giving him our whole lives. *"I appeal to you therefore, brothers, by the mercies of God, to present your bodies as a living sacrifice, holy and acceptable to God, which is your spiritual worship,"* **(Romans 12.1 ESV)**.

We worship through prayer. *"I urge, then, first of all, that petitions, prayers, intercession and thanksgiving be made for all people,"* **(1 Timothy 2.1 NIV)**.

We worship through reading and teaching the Bible. *"Let the word of Christ dwell in you richly, teaching and admonishing one another in all wisdom, singing psalms and hymns and spiritual songs, with thankfulness in your hearts to God,"* **(Colossians 3.16 ESV)**.

We worship through Communion. *"He took some bread and gave thanks to God for it. Then he broke it in pieces and gave it to the disciples, saying, 'This is my body, which is given for you. Do this in remembrance of me,'"* **(Luke 22.19 NLT)**. Communion is a remembrance of the death of Jesus. As we eat the bread and drink from the cup, we remember His sacrifice on the cross and His great love for us.

THINK IT OUT

What stood out to you most about worship today?

___
___
___
___
___
___
___
___
___
___

What questions do you have about *"gathered"* worship?

_____
_____
_____
_____
_____

Do you make weekly worship a priority? If, not, why not?

_____
_____
_____
_____
_____

LIVE IT OUT

Review your Scripture memory verse for the week:

"You are no longer foreigners and strangers, but fellow citizens with God's people and also members of his household."
(EPHESIANS 2.19 NIV)

Review your *"I Will"* statement for this week.

Read **(Luke 22:47-62)**. Continue to **l.i.s.t.e.n.** to God as you read and **p.r.a.y.**

PRAY IT OUT

Pray for those in your church that lead you to worship God.

DAY FOUR JOURNAL ENTRY

Look. **I**dentify. **S**tudy. **T**hink deeply. **E**ngage in prayer. **N**ote what God says.

Praise. **R**eturn. **A**sk. **Y**ield.

WEEK SEVEN · DAY FIVE

A PLACE TO CARE

We live in the technology age. We have access to information at the touch of a finger. Our culture says, *"I know."* Yet, despite all our knowledge, we struggle to find and experience real, lasting community.

The early church was a caring place. People met each other's needs. They prayed for each other and encouraged each other as they faced life's struggles. They were bonded together with a mutual love for Jesus and love for each other. They were a people on a mission, committed to sharing the gospel in their time. This love they expressed was something completely unlike the culture in which they lived.

Our culture says, *"I know,"* but biblical community says, *"I care."* The Apostle Paul spoke about this to the church at Rome. *"Let love be genuine. Abhor what is evil; hold fast to what is good. Love one another with brotherly affection. Outdo one another in showing honor. Do not be slothful in zeal, be fervent in spirit, serve the Lord. Rejoice in hope, be patient in tribulation, be constant in prayer. Contribute to the needs of the saints and seek to show hospitality. Bless those who persecute you; bless and do not curse them. Rejoice with those who rejoice, weep with those who weep. Live in harmony with one another,"* **(Romans 12.9-16 ESV)**. This is such a beautiful picture of what the church is called to be — a caring community.

Paul said a caring church is a place that says:

I care about you.
"Let love be genuine. Abhor what is evil; hold fast to what is good. Love one another with brotherly affection. Outdo one another in showing honor," **(Romans 12.9-10 ESV)**. Our love shouldn't be surface or fake, but real and genuine. It's a love that hates it when evil comes into someone's life, but celebrates and cheers when good is on display. It's a place where honor and brotherly affection are clear and compelling. In a world that is constantly pulling you down, God's community is committed to building you up, encouraging you, and bringing out the best in you.

I care about your needs.
"Contribute to the needs of the saints and seek to show hospitality," **(Romans 12.13 ESV)**. Members of the early church weren't only concerned with a person's spiritual life; they were concerned with the everyday practical life as well. If you had financial needs, they would help. If you were sick, they would care for you. If you needed a place to stay, their doors were open. Today should be no different. Real community cares for practical needs.

I care about your highs and your lows.
"Rejoice with those who rejoice, weep with those who weep," **(Romans 12.15 ESV)**. This moves us to an even deeper level of community. It's one thing to care about a person and even to care about their needs, but it's another thing to say, *"What makes you joyful makes me joyful; what makes you grieve makes me grieve!"* When you get a new job, have a new baby, mark that anniversary, I'm going to celebrate with you. When you are hurting, grieving, crying or doubting, I'll be there too. **(1 Corinthians 12.26 NASB)** says, *"And if one member suffers, all the members suffer with it; if one member is honored, all the members rejoice with it."*

THINK IT OUT

How have you experienced community like this?

_____
_____
_____
_____
_____
_____
_____

What keeps us from living like this today?

_____
_____
_____
_____
_____

What one thing could you do to show care and concern to someone in your church?

___

LIVE IT OUT

Review your Scripture memory verse for the week:

"You are no longer foreigners and strangers, but fellow citizens with God's people and also members of his household."
(EPHESIANS 2.19 NIV)

Review your *"I Will"* statement for this week.

Read **(Luke 23:26-49)**. Continue to **l.i.s.t.e.n.** to God as you read and **p.r.a.y.**

PRAY IT OUT

Pray for those in your church that lead you to worship God.

DAY FIVE JOURNAL ENTRY

Look. **I**dentify. **S**tudy. **T**hink deeply. **E**ngage in prayer. **N**ote what God says.

Praise. **R**eturn. **A**sk. **Y**ield.

WEEK **SEVEN** · DAY **SIX**

A PLACE TO GROW

Healthy things grow. I have marks on a doorframe in our house where we charted the growth of our girls. Just outside my office window, I have an oak tree that has grown over the years. My yard grows. Animals grow. Organizations grow. Things that are healthy naturally grow. And the same is true spiritually. God wants you to grow in your walk with Him.

Many Christians believe that spiritual growth is mostly about learning more information. The truth is, spiritual growth is not just knowing more about Jesus. Spiritual growth is not just doing more for Jesus. Spiritual growth is living more like Jesus. God wants you to look and act like Jesus. **(1 John 2.6 NIV)** says, *"Whoever claims to live in him must live as Jesus did."* That's God's goal for you.

Still not convinced? **(Ephesians 4.13 ESV)** says that God wants to shape you into *"the measure of the stature of the fullness of Christ."* **(Romans 8.29 ESV)** says, *"For those whom he foreknew he also predestined to be conformed to the image of his Son."* The Apostle Paul told the church at Galatia that he was *"in the anguish of childbirth until Christ is formed in you,"* **(Galatians 4.19 ESV)**.

God loves you just the way you are, but He loves you too much to leave you the way you are. He wants you to grow up to live just like Jesus. How does that happen? Part of growing to be more like Jesus is being in an environment to grow. The bonsai tree stays small because it stays in a pot. If it were planted in the ground, it could put its roots down and grow. Many people are like the bonsai tree. They need to get in a new environment where they can put their roots down and grow spiritually, and the perfect environment for spiritual growth is the church.

A church is like a spiritual greenhouse where the conditions are optimal for spiritual growth. Why is the church the perfect place to grow?

You grow by learning to accept people who are different from you.
"Walk in a manner worthy of the calling to which you have been called, with all humility and gentleness, with patience, bearing with one another in love, eager to maintain the unity of the Spirit in the bond of peace," **(Ephesians 4.1-3 ESV)**. In the church, you learn to live with, and love people who are different from you. You learn to practice patience and gentleness. You learn to bear with others in love and maintain unity and peace.

You grow by learning from godly people.
"And he gave the apostles, the prophets, the evangelists, the shepherds and teachers ... for building up the body of Christ, until we all attain to the unity of the faith and of the knowledge of the Son of God, to mature manhood ... so that we may no longer be children, tossed to and fro by the waves and carried about by every wind of doctrine," **(Ephesians 4.11-14 ESV)**. In the church, God provides pastors and leaders, shepherds and teachers to train and equip each person to walk with God and serve Him. This way you don't have to stay spiritual infants, always needing someone to feed and care for you. You can grow to be mature men or women who can feed yourselves and help others in their spiritual journey.

You grow by serving.
Paul writes that the result of our spiritual growth is *"to equip the saints for the work of ministry,"* **(Ephesians 4.12 ESV)**. As you learn to serve others, you are learning to become more like Jesus, who came to be a servant. Jesus said about Himself, *"For even the Son of Man came not to be served but to serve others and to give his life as a ransom for many,"* **(Matthew 20.28 NLT)**.

THINK IT OUT

What is the measure of true spiritual growth?

_____
_____
_____
_____
_____
_____
_____

Describe a time when you grew spiritually?

_____
_____
_____
_____
_____

Are you participating in a group at church where you can grow? If not, why not?

_____
_____
_____
_____
_____
_____

LIVE IT OUT

Review your Scripture memory verse for the week:

"You are no longer foreigners and strangers, but fellow citizens with God's people and also members of his household."
(EPHESIANS 2.19 NIV)

Review your *"I Will"* statement for this week.

Read **(Luke 24:13-35)**. Continue to **l.i.s.t.e.n.** to God as you read and **p.r.a.y.**

PRAY IT OUT

Pray for God to grow you to full spiritual maturity.
Ask God to help you grow as you walk with Him every day.

DAY SIX JOURNAL ENTRY

Look. **I**dentify. **S**tudy. **T**hink deeply. **E**ngage in prayer. **N**ote what God says.

Praise. **R**eturn. **A**sk. **Y**ield.

WEEK **SEVEN** · DAY **SEVEN**

SEARCH AND RESCUE

Jesus came on a mission — a search and rescue mission. **(Luke 19.10 ESV)** says, *"For the Son of Man came to seek and to save the lost."* The metanarrative of the Bible — the sweeping panoramic view of Scripture — is that we were created for community with God and with each other. However, that community was ripped apart by sin, and Jesus came to restore what was broken by reconciling us to God and to each other.

We were lost, adrift from God, and Jesus plunged into our world and offered Himself to bring us back. **(1 Peter 3.18 NIV)** says, *"For Christ also suffered once for sins, the righteous for the unrighteous, to bring you to God."* Jesus' dream was that His people would live out that search and rescue mentality after He was gone.

Every healthy church has a search and rescue mentality. Every healthy community of believers is driven by the fact that there is someone tonight going to bed praying, *"God, if you are real, send someone to help me!"*

In Jesus' day, He was confronted with religious people who claimed to love God but were indifferent and unconcerned about people. One day, to drive home the point that people matter to God, He blasted off three rapid-fire stories to teach them a powerful lesson. Take a moment to read these stories found in Luke 15.4-24. These accounts are breathtaking because they remind us how God sees people who are far from Him.

He sees every person as valuable.
In every story, something valuable is *"lost."* The first story had a *"lost"* sheep. The second story had a *"lost"* coin. The last story had a *"lost"* son. In every story, something extremely valuable went missing! *What does this tell us?* It tells us how God feels about every person. Every person matters to God. To put it another way, you have never laid eyes on a person who doesn't matter to God. No matter the color of their skin, where they were raised, their education, their background, how good or bad they've been, how moral or immoral, how religious or irreligious — all people matter to God. It also tells us that people are *"lost."* We don't like to think of ourselves or anyone else as spiritually *"lost."* Many people think the term *"lost"* is outdated; even offensive. But this is the word Jesus used. While we are valuable in God's eyes, apart from Christ, we are *"lost."* **(Ephesians 2.12 NIV)** says that without Christ every one of us is *"without hope and without God in the world."* You know people just like that. They don't know who they are. They don't know where they are going. They don't know how to be right with God. They are drifting far from God. That is how God sees you and me apart from Him. Priceless, but lost.

He sees every person as worth rescuing.

Another similarity in each of these stories is that an all-out search was launched to recover what was lost. The shepherd went searching. The woman started sweeping and moving furniture. The father stood on the front porch watching. Jesus was saying: *"While people you know are valuable to me and are distant from me, I'm on a search and rescue mission for them!"* That's the heart of God. Jesus came *"to seek and save the lost,"* **(Luke 19.10 ESV)**. Jesus came for messed up people like you and me. **(John 3.17 NIV)** says, *"For God did not send his Son into the world to condemn the world, but to save the world through him."*

He sees every person as worth celebrating.

In every case, when that which was lost was found, there was a huge celebration! The shepherd came back with his lost sheep draped over his shoulders, and he called his friends to celebrate. The woman, when she found her lost coin, called her friends over and said, *"Celebrate with me, because my lost coin has been found."* After the father embraced his son, he told his servants to *"...bring the fattened calf and kill it, and let us eat and celebrate. For this my son was dead, and is alive again; he was lost, and is found.' And they began to celebrate,"* **(Luke 15.23-24 ESV)**. Listen, when anyone comes to faith in Jesus, it is cause for celebration!

This is how God sees people far from Him, and this is how He wants His people to see the people around them... valuable, worthy of being rescued, worthy of celebrating!

THINK IT OUT

Describe your *"search and rescue mentality"*.

_____
_____
_____
_____

What keeps you from having a *"search and rescue mentality"*?

_____
_____
_____
_____
_____

Who is one person you would like to see come to faith in Jesus?

___
___
___
___
___

LIVE IT OUT

Review your Scripture memory verse for the week:

"You are no longer foreigners and strangers, but fellow citizens with God's people and also members of his household."
(EPHESIANS 2.19 NIV)

Review your *"I Will"* statement for this week.

Take the day to review the notes you made through your reading in **Luke**. Reflect on what God has spoken to you.

PRAY IT OUT

Spend some time praying for one friend who is far from God.

Pray today for a few people you know that need to come to know and follow Jesus.

FOR GROUP TIME

*My **"I Will"** Statement:*

As a result of what I have just studied, I will put this one thing into practice this week:

DAY SEVEN JOURNAL ENTRY

Look. Identify. Study. Think deeply. Engage in prayer. Note what God says.

Praise. Return. Ask. Yield.

APPENDICES

II
HOW TO **L.I.S.T.E.N.** TO GOD'S VOICE

IV
HOW TO **P.R.A.Y.**

HOW TO L.I.S.T.E.N. TO GOD'S VOICE

"My sheep listen to my voice; I know them, and they follow me." — Jesus
(John 10.27, NIV)

God still speaks today, and those who follow Him listen to His voice. But how do you hear God's voice? God speaks primarily through His Word, the Bible. As you read the Bible and think deeply about what it says, applying it to your life, God speaks to you by His Spirit. Below is a simple way to **l.i.s.t.e.n.** to God's voice every day.

Look at a passage from God's Word. Listening begins with looking into God's Word. If God speaks primarily through His Word, then you need to read God's Word to hear from Him. Make it a habit to read God's Word every day. As you begin your reading each day, stop and pray. Ask God to open your eyes to see Him and open your ears to hear His Voice. Pray, *"Speak Lord; I'm listening to you."*

Identify what stands out. As you read, be sensitive to what the Spirit of God is pointing out for you to notice. Oftentimes, a word or phrase will stand out. Sometimes the Spirit will point out a teaching that directly applies to you. Don't read casually for content; read actively, looking for what God has for you that day. When verses stand out, underline or highlight them in your Bible.

Study God's truth. Now that you are focused on a few passages, study them. Look at them closely. Picture what is happening. Write down your observations. Use the **ACTS** guide to help you. Is there an *Attitude* to change, a *Command* to follow, a *Truth* to believe or a *Sin* to confess? Ask God to show you these things.

Think about how this applies to your life. Once you have a clear picture of the meaning, ponder it in your heart. Think deeply about how these truths apply to your life. This is what the Bible calls meditation. **(Psalm 119.15 NIV)** says, *"I meditate on your precepts and consider your ways."* God told Joshua, *"Study this Book of Instruction continually. Meditate on it day and night so you will be sure to obey everything written in it. Only then will you prosper and succeed in all you do,"* **(Joshua 1.8, NLT)**.

Engage with God in prayer. Now pray about what you just read, asking God to make it real in your own life. Oftentimes, simply praying the Scripture back to God in your own words is very powerful. If there is sin to confess, then confess it to Him quickly and receive His promised forgiveness, **(1 John 1.9 ESV)**.

Note what God has said in a journal. Over the years, great men and women of faith have participated in spiritual journaling as a pathway to knowing God better. Here are some practical tips as you begin to journal:

1) Date the page at the top so you will remember when God spoke to you.

2) Write down the key passage and any insights God gives you.

3) Record how this passage applies to your life.

4) Write down your personal prayer. Write as if you are writing a letter to Jesus.

5) Summarize what God has spoken to you in a short title and write it at the top of the page.

HOW TO P.R.A.Y.

"My heart says of you, 'Seek his face!' Your face, LORD, I will seek."
(Psalm 27.8 NIV)

God wants you to seek His face and know Him in a deep and personal way. Part of seeking God is speaking to Him in prayer. Jesus' disciples came to Him and asked Him how to pray. They knew that the secret to Jesus' fellowship with the Father and source of strength was in His prayer life. Jesus gave His disciples a model prayer to follow that would lead them into fellowship with the Father **(Matthew 6.9-13 ESV)**. Below is a simple way to **p.r.a.y.** like Jesus every day.

Praise. Jesus begins His prayer with praising the Father. *"Our Father in heaven, hallowed be your name"* **(Matthew 6.9 ESV)**. Hallowed means holy, set apart or to revere something or someone. Jesus is saying, *"Father, your name is holy!"* The first thing you need to do when you come into God's presence is praise. **(Psalm 100.4 NIV)** says, *"Enter his gates with thanksgiving and his courts with praise; give thanks to him and praise his name."* **(Psalm 22.3 ESV)** says *"Yet you are holy, enthroned on the praises of Israel.* The angels are in God's presence crying out, *"Holy, holy, holy is the LORD Almighty; the whole earth is full of his glory,"* **(Isaiah 6.3 NIV)**. When you come into God's presence, don't come in with your hands out asking for something; come with you hands up praising Him!

Return. Next Jesus prayed, *"Your Kingdom come, your will be done, on earth as it is in heaven,"* **(Matthew 6.10 ESV)**. Why did Jesus pray for the kingdom to come? The kingdom of God is the rule of God in the lives of His people. To be a part of God's kingdom is to do His will. Those who do God's will are part of His kingdom. When you pray, *"Your kingdom come, your will be done,"* you are praying *"Father, right now, I want you to rule in my life."* But as soon as we pray that, we have to confess that we don't really live that way. There are many areas of our lives where we go outside of God's will. We sin. We fail. We struggle. We wander. That's why we need to return to the Lord. This is the time to ask God to search your heart and show you your sin **(Psalm 139.23 ESV)**, and then quickly confess it to Him **(1 John 1.9 ESV)**.

Ask. God wants you to come to Him and ask Him for the things you need. Jesus said, *"Keep on asking, and you will receive what you ask for. Keep on seeking, and you will find. Keep on knocking, and the door will be opened to you. For everyone who asks, receives. Everyone who seeks, finds. And to everyone who knocks, the door will be opened,"* **(Matthew 7.7-8 NLT)**. Jesus asked His Father for several things, and in prayer, you can ask for these same things. Ask for God's provision: *"Give us this day our daily bread,"* **(Matthew 6.11 ESV)**. Ask for God's best in your relationships: *"forgive us our debts, as we also have forgiven our debtors"* **(Matthew 6.12 ESV)**. Ask for God's protection: *"And lead us not into temptation, but deliver us from evil,"* **(Matthew 6.13 ESV)**.

Yield. Jesus closed His prayer by yielding His whole heart and life to the Father. *"[For yours is the kingdom and the power and the glory, forever. Amen,]"* **(Matthew 6.13 NASB)**. Just as a yield sign indicates you should let someone else go ahead of you, in our walk with God, yield means we surrender our whole lives to Jesus and commit to follow His lead. Yielding means acknowledging Jesus' authority in your life, surrendering to the Spirit's leadership and giving God glory in everything you do.

We Exist to Empower Church Leaders
to Live, Lead, & Leverage Their Influence
to Ignite Movements of Multiplication.

discipleFIRST.com

Experience Continual Growth
With Your Ministry Team
Through Training On-Demand

Learn More at discipleFIRST.com/hub